FAVORITE
FRUITCAKES

BOOKS BY MOIRA HODGSON

✂

Good Food from a Small Kitchen

The Hot and Spicy Cookbook

Keeping Company: Contemporary Menus
for Delicious Food and Relaxed Entertaining

Quintet: Five American Dance Companies

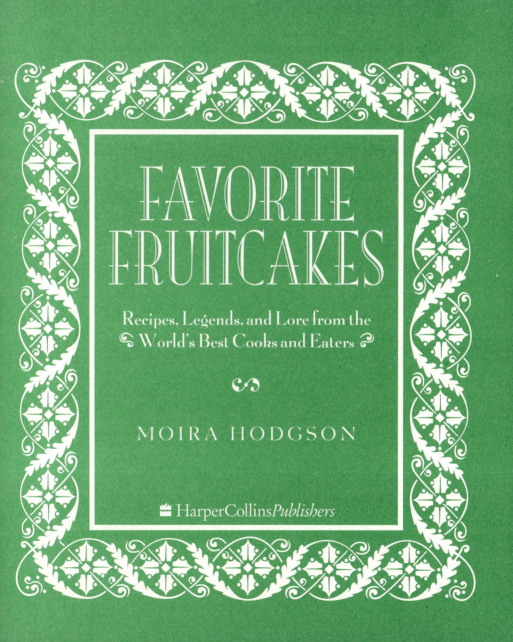

FAVORITE FRUITCAKES

Recipes, Legends, and Lore from the
World's Best Cooks and Eaters

MOIRA HODGSON

HarperCollins*Publishers*

FAVORITE FRUITCAKES. Copyright © 1993 by Moira Hodgson. All rights reserved. Printed in the United States of America. No part of this book may be used or reproduced in any manner whatsoever without written permission except in the case of brief quotations embodied in critical articles and reviews. For information address HarperCollins Publishers, Inc., 10 East 53rd Street, New York, NY 10022.

HarperCollins books may be purchased for educational, business, or sales promotional use. For information please write: Special Markets Department, HarperCollins Publishers, Inc., 10 East 53rd Street, New York, NY 10022.

FIRST EDITION

DESIGNED BY JOEL AVIROM

Decorative borders by Laura Wilson

LIBRARY OF CONGRESS CATALOGING-IN-PUBLICATION DATA

Hodgson, Moira.
    Favorite fruitcakes : recipes, legends, and lore from the world's best cooks and eaters / Moira Hodgson.
        p.   cm.
    Includes bibliographical references and index.
    ISBN 0-06-016942-7
    1. Fruitcake. I. Title.
TX771.H63   1993   92-56213
641.8'653—dc20

93 94 95 96 97 ❖RRD❖ 10 9 8 7 6 5 4 3 2 1

Contents

LIGHT FRUITCAKES

FAVORITE EUROPEAN FRUITCAKES

I would like to thank my family and friends, who not only supplied me with ideas and sources for fruitcake recipes but happily ate fruitcake while I was working on this book.
I also thank my editor, Susan Friedland, whose idea it was to write a book on fruitcakes, and my agent Robert Cornfield.

ॐ

INTRODUCTION

ԑℑ

People either love fruitcakes or hate them, the latter I think because they know only the commercial variety—heavy, dried-out cakes made with supermarket candied fruits that are dyed alarming colors and often have a strange, soapy taste. But a real fruitcake is to store-bought ones what Camembert is to artificially flavored cheese spread, or Puligny Montrachet to white wine cooler.

I happen to love a well-made fruitcake. Just the smell of one reminds me of my English childhood. We often had fruitcakes for afternoon tea—Dundee cakes topped with almonds, light spongy fruitcakes laced with raisins and walnuts, and rich dark fruitcakes aged for months and sent along by relatives for the holidays.

Most of all, fruitcakes for me were a reminder of home. As a child, I invariably spent Christmas abroad since my father was in the Foreign Service and we changed countries every couple of years. We were often so far from England that returning home for Christmas holidays was out of the question. And Christmas in Saigon, Beirut, or even Stockholm just wasn't the same without a fruitcake that had been aged for a month or two in the mail, and a tree hung with the tarnished Christmas decorations that had followed us halfway around the world.

Those who believe there is only one fruitcake and that its best function is as a doorstop will be surprised by the variety of cakes in this book. To choose the recipes, I researched dozens of cookbooks and asked friends and family for their favorites. I chose some cakes because they sounded unusual and appealing, others because I admired the chefs who had baked them, and subsequently found them to be tried and true. There are fruitcakes made with Guinness, bourbon, sherry, or rum. They can include such unexpected ingredients as dried cherries, cranberries, ricotta cheese, chocolate, or espresso coffee.

The secret to a good fruitcake is the same as the secret to any good cooking: ingredients. They should be of the best quality (and that, unfortunately, means expensive). You don't, however, have to be a skilled baker to produce a good cake. You can improvise with fruits and nuts without doing anything drastic to the texture or necessarily wrecking the recipe. You don't have to put in ingredients if you don't like them, or you don't have them on hand. For example, in making a cake that required glacéed cherries, I couldn't get any when I needed them, so I used dried cherries instead. The result was delicious. If you don't like dates or walnuts, leave them out, or substitute fruits or nuts you do like. Fruitcake is forgiving; mistakes (unless they are grave ones, like forgetting to add the eggs) generally don't show.

You can spread the work out over a few days. You can do the required chopping of fruits and nuts on the first day and start soaking them in liquor as the recipe indicates. Even though many recipes call for finely chopped nuts, I find that walnuts and pecans added in halves slice easily once the cake is baked.

Baker Ken Haedrich puts both chopped fruits and nuts into a large bowl two days before he cooks the cake and adds honey, molasses, or maple syrup (whatever the recipe requires), along with the spices and lemon or orange peel. He lets this mixture sit for two nights, covered, in a cool place. He prepares the pans on the second day and the third day is for making the batter and putting everything together.

For a good smooth batter, the eggs and butter should be at room temperature. When the fruits are stirred in, you can follow the British tradition by making your holiday wish as you stir. The pans should be three-quarters full with batter and placed in the center of a preheated oven.

It is important not to overbake a fruitcake or it will be dry and crumbly instead of moist and soft. As soon as it begins to pull away from the sides of the pan, it should be removed from the oven. (To keep fruitcakes moist, Carole Walter suggests putting a pan of hot water in the oven while they are baking; this works very well. You can also put a strip of foil on top to stop them from drying out). When you put a cake tester into the middle of the cake it should not come out with uncooked batter on it, but it can be slightly sticky from the fruit. The top of the cake should be browned nicely and the cake shrunk slightly from the sides of the pan. It should cool in the pan. If the cake is too dry, an extra glass of rum or brandy poured over the top will usually remedy the situation. (One way to help make sure that fruitcake remains moist is to marinate the fruit and nuts in liquor for two or three days before you bake the cake.)

The cakes in this book are different shapes and sizes, so I have included servings for each recipe. Some of the cakes are very dense and rich, and an eight-inch one will feed twice as many as the same size cake in a lighter version.

Fruitcakes are easy to mail. Put them first in tins and then in boxes lined with layers of tissue paper. (At least with fruitcake, you don't have the same worries as mailing other foods. One winter when I was living in Mexico, I received a parcel of delicacies a kind friend thought I would be missing in the remote mountain village where I was staying. His package took six months to arrive. It contained, among other things, a wheel of Brie.)

In researching this book I tasted more fruitcakes in one year than most people probably eat in a lifetime. But I never got tired of them.

One Christmas when I was a little girl, an elderly aunt received a fruitcake. She told me she would take a slice a month, never more, for she was not allowed alcohol. After she cut her slice, she drenched the cloth in brandy and rewrapped the cake. Several years later, after she died, I found a small piece of wrapped fruitcake in a corner of her dinette. She had enjoyed that cake for the last three years of her life.

Marlene Sorosky, *Season's Greetings*

FRUITCAKE IS FOREVER

by Russell Baker

❧

Thirty-four years ago, I inherited the family fruitcake. Fruitcake is the only food durable enough to become a family heirloom. It had been in my grandmother's possession since 1880, and she passed it to a niece in 1933.

Surprisingly, the niece, who had always seemed to detest me, left it to me in her will. There was the usual family backbiting when the will was read. Relatives grumbled that I had no right to the family fruitcake. Some whispered that I had "got to" the dying woman when she was *in extremis* and guided her hand while she altered her will.

Nothing could be more absurd, since my dislike of fruitcake is notorious throughout the family. This distaste dates from a Christmas dinner when, at the age of 15, I dropped a small piece of fruitcake and shattered every bone in my right foot.

I would have renounced my inheritance except for the sentiment of the thing, for the family fruitcake was the symbol of our family's roots. When my grandmother inherited it, it was already 86 years old, having been baked by her great-grandfather in 1794 as a Christmas gift for President George Washington.

Washington with his high-flown view of ethical standards for Government workers, sent it back with thanks, explaining that he thought it unseemly for presidents to accept gifts weighing more than 80 pounds, even though they were only eight inches in diameter. This, at any rate, is the family story, and you can take it for what it's worth, which probably isn't much.

There is no doubt, though, about the fruitcake's great age. Sawing into it six Christmases ago, I came across a fragment of a 1794 newspaper with an account of the lynching of a real-estate speculator in New York City.

Thinking the thing was a valuable antique, I rented bank storage and hired Brink's guards every Christmas to bring it out, carry it to the table and return it to the vault after dinner. The whole family, of course, now felt entitled to come for Christmas dinner.

People who have never eaten fruitcake may think that after 34 years of being gnawed at by assemblages of 25 to 30 diners my inheritance would have vanished. People who have eaten fruitcake will realize that it was still almost as intact as on the day George Washington first saw it. While an eon, as someone has observed, may be two people and a ham, a fruitcake is forever.

It was an antiques dealer who revealed this truth to me. The children had reached college age, the age of parental bankruptcy, and I decided to put the family fruitcake on the antiques market.

"Over 200 years old?" The dealer sneered. "I've got one at home that's *over* 300," he said. "If you come across a fruitcake that Julius Caesar brought back from Gaul, look me up; I'll give you $10 for it."

To cut expenses, I took it out of the bank. Still, there was that backbreaking cost of feeding 25 to 30 relatives each Christmas when they felt entitled to visit the family fruitcake. An idea was born.

Before leaving town for a weekend I placed it on the television set. When burglars came for the TV, they were bound to think the antique fruitcake worth a fortune and have it in some faraway pawnshop before discovering the truth.

By Monday morning the television was gone, all right, but the fruitcake was still with us. "I should have wired it," I told Uncle Jimmy. "Burglars won't take anything that isn't electronic these days."

Uncle Jimmy was not amused. "You're a lucky man," he said.

Lucky? Bankrupted by an idiotic faith in higher education was what I was.

"Lucky!" he shouted. "Don't you know there's a curse on the family fruitcake? It is said that a dreadful fate will fall upon anyone who lets the family fruitcake pass out of the possession of the family."

That didn't really scare me. Still, it couldn't hurt to play safe. After that, I kept the fruitcake locked in the crawl space under the kitchen. This afternoon, I shall bring it out again when 25 to 30 relatives come to dinner, and afterward we will all groan as people always groan when their interiors feel clogged with cement.

I now suspect Uncle Jimmy of lying about the curse. I suspect the dreadful fate carried by the family fruitcake is visited upon the one who inherits it. I wish I had a relative in the higher education business so I could will it to him.

The New York Times Magazine, December 25, 1983

IN DEFENSE OF FRUITCAKE

Are you, dear friend, one of the chosen, the enlightened, the few—who enjoys a good fruitcake, chock full of the freshest pecans and candied cherries and pineapple, bound only by ounces of deliciously spiced and perhaps liquored cake batter? Then bless you!

Or are you, poor soul, the one who spouts at the mention of fruitcake, "makes a damn good doorstop" or "I hope Aunt Ruth brings her fruitcake this year, ha-ha, we need another football!" Then shame on you!

In 1976, when I opened my first bakery, at age 27, I will admit that I had my reservations about fruitcake. I was young, inexperienced, and although I'd been exposed to quality fruitcake baking I had not yet "discovered" fruitcake. I may have even, at some time in my life, given in to "fruitcake bashing" myself, joining in with the legion of misguided individuals who smear fruitcake, the naive, the palateless.

Five minutes ago, here at 3:30 A.M., I turned by hand 100 pounds of beautiful cherries, pineapple, pecans, walnuts, and blanched almonds into rum flavor and rum—to soak, and to be used later as the fruitcake topping. The sight of the fruit mixture and the aroma of the flavors are more than heavenly. I know my assistant, Mary, will arrive shortly and exclaim in a kind of low, sensual tone, "OHHHHH!—Are we making fruitcake today?"

So what'sa matter? How did fruitcake acquire so many foes? Folks who are assured that most people in the group will agree with them as they wince and moan and gesture their fingers down their throats that fruitcake makes a better paperweight than food . . . ?

Years ago when Aunt Ruth and millions of Aunt Ruths like her were shopping for their fruitcake ingredients, they found something new on the shelf. Something pretty, something inexpensive . . . candied citrus peel! "Wouldn't that make a fine addition to my fruitcake," thought Ruth, "and so inexpensive!" And so on that day millions of pretty, but pretty awful fruitcakes were born.

Marvelous little packages, those canned Currier and Ives–embossed hostess gifts masquerading as fruitcake. Those mountains of chain-store gift boxes for the purveyors of the fruitcake myth. The perfectly merchandised two-pound cans of batter-laced citron, ready to go for $2.99.

In our business, we sell hundreds of "real" fruitcake each holiday season. I would like to offer several suggestions if you intend to treat yourself to an authentic fruitcake this year.

1. Try to find an independent baker whose reputation depends on quality "good things to eat."
2. Be prepared to pay at least $5.00 per pound for a good fruitcake.
3. Chill it before slicing.
4. Serve it ceremoniously, sliced thin, with a quality coffee or tea.

Fruitcake, misunderstood and stripped of its former stature by greed and corporate merchandising, needs our help! Enjoy a good fruitcake, and invite some friends. And don't forget to buy one for Aunt Ruth!

—Richard Seaberg, President
Richard's Bakery, Portland, Oregon
(written for the Retail Bakers Association of America)

DARK
FRUITCAKES

In my opinion, dark fruitcakes are the Rolls-Royces of the genre. They age like good wine and acquire their rich, dark color from such ingredients as dark brown sugar, molasses, espresso coffee, or melted bitter chocolate. Most in this chapter are soaked in spirits, wrapped in cheesecloth, and kept in a cool dark place to age for a month or two before the holidays. They are so rich that a very small slice is usually an ample portion and they can be made in small loaves for holiday gifts.

A dark fruitcake can be a luxurious sight, as is Julia Child's, which is painted with apricot glaze and decorated with glacéed cherries and nut meats. Chocolate fruitcakes are also festive, and something of an exotic novelty. Chocolate goes very well with unsweetened dried fruits—and with brandy and rum.

For people who don't like glacéed fruit, there are great dark fruitcakes made only with dried or fresh fruits. Nowadays, it is possible to get all manner of interesting dried fruits with which you can improvise. Dried cherries, blueberries, and cranberries, sold in specialty and health food stores, are among my favorites.

For dark fruitcakes to age properly they should be wrapped in muslin or cheesecloth that has been soaked in spirits such as brandy, rum, or whiskey and stored in airtight containers or wrapped well in aluminum foil. The cloths should be moistened once a month and replaced every three or four months. They should be stored in a cool place—not the refrigerator.

A CHRISTMAS MEMORY
by Truman Capote

ↄ

Imagine a morning in late November. A coming of winter morning more than twenty years ago. Consider the kitchen of a spreading old house in a country town. A great black stove is its main feature; but there is also a big round table and a fireplace with two rocking chairs placed in front of it. Just today the fireplace commenced its seasonal roar.

A woman with shorn white hair is standing at the kitchen window. She is wearing tennis shoes and a shapeless gray sweater over a summery calico dress. She is small and sprightly, like a bantam hen; but, due to a long youthful illness, her shoulders are pitifully hunched. Her face is remarkable—not unlike Lincoln's, craggy like that, and tinted by sun and wind; but it is delicate too, finely boned, and her eyes are sherry-colored and timid. "Oh my," she exclaims, her breath smoking the windowpane, "it's fruitcake weather!"

The person to whom she is speaking is myself. I am seven; she is sixty-something. We are cousins, very distant ones, and we have lived together—well, as long as I can remember. Other people inhabit the house, relatives; and though they have power over us, and frequently make us cry, we are not, on the whole, too much aware of them. We are each other's best friend. She calls me Buddy, in memory of a boy who was formerly her best friend. The other Buddy died in the 1880s, when she was still a child. She is still a child.

"I knew it before I got out of bed" she says, turning away from the window with a purposeful excitement in her eyes. "The courthouse bell sounded so cold and clear. And there were no birds singing; they've gone to warmer country, yes indeed. Oh, Buddy, stop stuffing biscuit and fetch our buggy. Help me find my hat. We've thirty cakes to bake."

It's always the same: a morning arrives in November, and my friend, as though officially inaugurating the Christmas time of year that exhilarates her imagination and fuels the blaze of her heart, announces: "It's fruitcake weather! Fetch our buggy. Help me find my hat."

The hat is found, a straw cartwheel corsaged with velvet roses out-of-doors has faded: it once belonged to a more fashionable relative. Together, we guide our buggy, a dilapidated baby carriage, out to the garden and into a grove of pecan trees. The buggy is mine: that is, it was bought for me when I was born. It is made of wicker, rather unraveled, and the wheels wobble like a drunkard's legs. But it is a faithful object; springtimes, we take it to the woods and fill it with flowers, herbs, wild fern for our porch pots; in the summer we pile it with picnic paraphernalia and sugar-cane fishing poles and roll it down to the edge of a creek; it has its winter uses, too: as a truck for hauling firewood from the yard to the kitchen, as a warm bed for Queenie, our tough little orange and white rat terrier who has survived distemper and two rattlesnake bites. Queenie is trotting beside it now.

Three hours later we are back in the kitchen hauling a heaping buggyload of windfall pecans. Our backs hurt from gathering them: how hard they were to find (the main crop having been shaken off the trees and sold by the orchard's owners, who are not us) among the concealing leaves, the frosted, deceiving grass. Caarackle! A cheery crunch, scraps of miniature thunder sound as the shells collapse and the golden mound of sweet oily ivory meat mounts in the milk-glass bowl. Queenie begs to taste, and now and again my friend sneaks her a mite, though insisting  we deprive ourselves. "We mustn't, Buddy. If we start, we won't stop. And there's scarcely enough as it is. For thirty cakes." The kitchen is growing dark. Dusk turns the window into a mirror: our reflections mingle with the rising moon as we work by the fireside in the firelight. At last, when the moon is quite high we toss the final hull into the fire and, with joined sighs, watch it catch flame. The buggy is empty, the bowl is brimful.

We eat our supper (cold biscuits, bacon, blackberry jam) and discuss tomorrow. Tomorrow the kind of work I like best begins: buying. Cherries and citron, ginger and vanilla and canned Hawaiian pineapple, rinds and raisins and walnuts and whiskey and oh, so much flour, butter, so many eggs, spices, flavorings: why, we'll need a pony to pull the buggy home.

But before these purchases can be made, there is the question of money. Neither of us has any. Except for skinflint sums persons in the house occasionally provide (a dime is considered very big money); or what we earn ourselves from various activities: holding rummage sales, selling buckets of hand-picked blackberries, jars of homemade jam and apple jelly and peach preserves, rounding up flowers for funerals and weddings. Once we won seventy-ninth prize, five dollars, in a national football contest. Not that we know a fool thing about football. It's just that we enter any contest we hear about: at the moment our hopes are centered on the fifty-thousand-dollar Grand Prize being offered to name a new brand of coffee (we suggested "A.M."; and, after some hesitation, for my friend thought it perhaps sacrilegious, the slogan "A.M.! Amen!"). To tell the truth, our only *really* profitable enterprise was the Fun and Freak Museum we conducted in a backyard woodshed two summers ago. The Fun was a stereopticon with slide views of Washington and New York lent to us by a relative who had been to those places (she was furious when she discovered why we'd borrowed it); the Freak was a three-legged biddy chicken hatched by one of our own hens. Everybody hereabouts wanted to see that biddy: we charged grownups a nickel, kids two cents. And took in a good twenty dollars before the museum shut down due to the decease of the main attraction.

But one way and another we do each year accumulate Christmas savings, a Fruitcake Fund. These moneys we keep hidden in an ancient bead purse under a loose board under the floor under a chamber pot under my friend's bed. The purse is seldom removed from this safe location except to make a deposit, or, as happens every Saturday, a withdrawal; for on Saturdays I am allowed ten cents to go to the picture show. My friend has never been to a picture show, nor does she intend to: "I'd rather hear you tell the story, Buddy. That way I can imagine it more. Besides, a person my age shouldn't squander their eyes. When the Lord comes, let me see Him clear." In addition to never having seen a movie, she has never: eaten in a restaurant, traveled more than five miles from home, received or sent a telegram, read anything except funny papers and the Bible, worn cosmetics, cursed, wished someone harm, told a lie on purpose, let a hungry dog go hungry. Here are a few things she has done, does do: killed with a hoe the biggest rattlesnake ever seen in this county (sixteen rattles), dip snuff (secretly), tame hummingbirds (just try it) till they balance on her finger, tell ghost stories (we both believe in ghosts) so tingling they chill you in July, talk to herself, take walks in the rain, grow the prettiest japonicas in town, know the recipe for every sort of old-time Indian cure, including a magical wart-remover.

Now, with supper finished, we retire to the room in a faraway part of the house where my friend sleeps in a scrap-quilt-covered iron bed painted rose pink, her favorite color. Silently, wallowing in the pleasures of conspiracy, we take the bead purse from its secret place and spill its contents on the scrap quilt. Dollar bills, tightly rolled and green as May buds. Somber fifty-cent pieces, heavy enough to weight a dead man's eyes. Lovely dimes, the liveliest coin, the one that really jingles. Nickels and quarters, worn smooth as creek pebbles. But mostly a hateful heap of bitter-odored pennies. Last summer others in the house contracted to pay us a penny for every twenty-five flies we killed. Oh the carnage of August: the flies that flew to heaven! Yet it was not work in which we took pride. And, as we sit counting pennies, it is as though we were back tabulating dead flies. Neither of us has a head for figures; we count slowly, lose track, start again. According to her calculations, we have $12.73. According to mine, exactly $13. "I do hope you're wrong, Buddy. We can't mess around with thirteen. The cakes will fall. Or put somebody in the cemetery. Why, I wouldn't dream of getting out of bed on the thirteenth." This is true: she always spends thirteenths in bed. So, to be on the safe side, we subtract a penny and toss it out the window.

Of the ingredients that go into our fruitcakes, whiskey is the most expensive, as well as the hardest to obtain: State laws forbid its sale. But everyone knows you can buy a bottle from Mr. Haha Jones. And the next day, having completed our more prosaic shopping, we set out for Mr. Haha's business address, a "sinful" (to quote public opinion) fish-fry and dancing café down by the river. We've been there before, and on the same errand; but in previous years our dealings have been with Haha's wife, an iodine-dark Indian woman with brassy peroxided hair and a dead-tired disposition. Actually, we've never laid eyes on her husband, though we've heard that he's an Indian too. A giant with razor scars across his cheeks. They call him Haha because he's so gloomy, a man who never laughs. As we approach his café (a large log cabin festooned inside and out with chains of garish-gay naked light bulbs and standing by the river's muddy edge under the shade of river trees where moss drifts through the branches like gray mist) our steps slow down. Even Queenie stops prancing and sticks close by. People have been murdered in Haha's café. Cut to pieces. Hit on the head. There's a case coming up in court next month. Naturally these goings-on happen at night when the colored lights cast crazy patterns and the victrola wails. In the daytime Haha's is shabby and deserted. I knock at the door, Queenie barks, my friend calls: "Mrs. Haha, ma'am? Anyone to home?"

Footsteps. The door opens. Our hearts overturn. It's Mr. Haha Jones himself! And he *is* a giant; he *does* have scars; he *doesn't* smile. No, he glowers at us through Satan-tilted eyes and demands to know: "What you want with Haha?"

For a moment we are too paralyzed to tell. Presently my friend half-finds her voice, a whispery voice at best: "If you please, Mr. Haha, we'd like a quart of your finest whiskey."

His eyes tilt more. Would you believe it? Haha is smiling! Laughing, too. "Which one of you is a drinkin' man?"

"It's for making fruitcakes, Mr. Haha. Cooking."

This sobers him. He frowns. "That's no way to waste good whiskey." Nevertheless, he retreats into the shadowed café and seconds later appears carrying a bottle of daisy-yellow unlabeled liquor. He demonstrates its sparkle in the sunlight and says: "Two dollars."

We pay him with nickels and dimes and pennies. Suddenly, as he jangles the coins in his hand like a fistful of dice, his face softens. "Tell you what," he proposes, pouring the money back into our bead purse, "just send me one of them fruitcakes instead."

"Well," my friend remarks on our way home, "there's a lovely man. We'll put an extra cup of raisins in his cake."

The black stove, stoked with coal and firewood, glows like a lighted pumpkin. Eggbeaters whirl, spoons spin round in bowls of butter and sugar, vanilla sweetens the air, ginger spices it; melting, nose-tingling odors saturate the kitchen, suffuse the house, drift out to the world on puffs of chimney smoke. In four days our work is done. Thirty-one cakes, dampened with whiskey, bask on window sills and shelves.

Who are they for?

Friends. Not necessarily neighbor friends: indeed, the larger share is intended for persons we've met maybe once, perhaps not at all. People who've struck our fancy. Like President Roosevelt. Like the Reverend and Mrs. J.C. Lucey, Baptist missionaries to Borneo who lectured here last winter. Or the little knife grinder who comes through town twice a year. Or Abner Packer, the driver of the six o'clock bus from Mobile who exchanges waves with us every day as he passes in a dust-cloud whoosh.

Or the young Wistons, a California couple whose car one afternoon broke down outside the house and spent a pleasant hour chatting with us on the porch (young Mr. Wiston snapped our picture, the only one we've ever had taken). Is it because my friend is shy with everyone *except* strangers that these strangers, and merest acquaintances, seem to us our truest friends? I think yes. Also, the scrapbooks we keep of thank-you's on White House stationery, time-to-time communications from California and Borneo, the knife grinder's penny postcards, make us feel connected to eventful worlds beyond the kitchen with its view of a sky that stops.

Now a nude December fig branch grates against the window. The kitchen is empty, the cakes are gone; yesterday we carted the last of them to the post office, where the cost of stamps turned our purse inside out. We're broke. That rather depresses me but my friend insists on celebrating—with two inches of whiskey left in Haha's bottle. Queenie has a spoonful in a bowl of coffee (she likes her coffee chicory flavored and strong). The rest we divide between a pair of jelly glasses. We're both quite awed at the prospect of drinking straight whiskey; the taste of it brings screwed-up expressions and sour shoulders. But by and by we begin to sing, the two of us singing different songs simultaneously. I don't know the words to mine just: *Come on along, come on along, to the dark-town strutters' ball.* But I can dance: that's what I mean to be, a tap-dancer in the movies. My dancing shadow rollicks on the walls; our voices rock the chinaware; we giggle: as if unseen hands were tickling us. Queenie rolls on her back, her paws in the air, something like a grin stretches her black lips. Inside myself, I feel warm and sparky as those crumbling logs, carefree as the wind in the chimney. My friend waltzes round the stove, the hem of her poor calico skirt pinched between her fingers as though it were a party dress: *Show me the way to go home,* she sings, her tennis shoes squeaking on the floor. *Show me the way to go home.*

Enter: two relatives. Very Angry. Potent with eyes that scold, tongues that scald. Listen to what they have to say, the words tumbling together into a wrathful tune: "A child of seven! whiskey on his breath! must be loony! road to ruination! remember Cousin Kate? Uncle Charlie? Uncle Charlie's brother-in-law? shame! scandal! humiliation! kneel, pray, beg the Lord!"

Queenie sneaks under the stove. My friend gazes at her shoes, her chin quivers, she lifts her skirt and blows her nose and runs to her room. Long after the town has gone to sleep and the house is silent except for the chimings of clocks and the sputter of fading fires, she is weeping into a pillow already as wet as a widow's handkerchief.

"Don't cry," I say, sitting at the bottom of her bed and shivering despite my flannel nightgown that smells of last winter's cough syrup; "don't cry," I beg, teasing her toes, tickling her feet, "you're too old for that."

"It's because," she hiccups, "I *am* too old. Old and funny."

"Not funny. Fun. More fun than anybody. Listen. If you don't stop crying you'll be so tired tomorrow we can't go out and cut a tree."

She straightens up. Queenie jumps on the bed (where Queenie is not allowed) to lick her cheeks. "I know where we'll find real pretty trees, Buddy. And holly too. With berries as big as your eyes. It's way off in the woods. Farther than we've ever been. Papa used to bring us Christmas trees from there: carry them on his shoulder. That's fifty years ago. Well, now: I can't wait for morning."

JAMES BEARD'S MOTHER'S BLACK FRUITCAKE

෴

This fruitcake contains filberts and grated chocolate. It should be stored in cheesecloth soaked in Cognac.

"When the cake was just warm from the oven," wrote Beard, "Mother used to add a bath of Cognac and put the cakes in tins to rest till they were to be used. She would make five times this recipe every year and often keep the cakes through the year with towels dampened in Cognac wrapped around them, and in airtight containers, of course. This recipe was also used for wedding cakes."

1½ cups citron, cut into thin
    shreds
1 cup orange peel, cut into thin
    shreds
3 cups candied pineapple, cut into
    thin shreds
1½ cups glacéed cherries, cut in
    half
4 cups seedless raisins
2 cups sultanas
2 cups currants
1¼ cups Cognac, plus additional
    for brushing and for soaking
    cheesecloth

2 cups filberts
3 cups flour
1 teaspoon ground cinnamon
Pinch of ground cloves
½ teaspoon ground mace
Pinch of grated nutmeg
½ teaspoon baking soda
8 tablespoons (1 stick) unsalted
    butter
2 cups sugar (part brown sugar
    may be used)
6 eggs, lightly beaten
3 ounces unsweetened chocolate,
    grated

1. Combine the citron, orange peel, pineapple, cherries, raisins, sultanas, and currants. Add 1 cup of the Cognac to this mixture, cover, and let sit in the refrigerator for 2 days.
2. Toast the filberts in a 350-degree oven for 30 minutes. Coarsely chop them or leave them whole, as you wish.
3. On the day you bake the cake, remove the fruit from the refrigerator, sprinkle ½ cup sifted flour over it, and blend the mixture well. Add the nuts and mix again.
4. Sift the remaining 2½ cups flour and then measure to exactly 2½ cups. Combine the flour with the cinnamon, cloves, mace, and nutmeg. Add the baking soda.
5. Preheat the oven to 275 degrees. Line a pan or pans with wax paper or brown paper. If you use brown paper you will need to butter the pans first. I use 9-inch bread pans, 1 large square pan, or two 9-inch springforms.
6. Cream together the butter and sugar. Add the eggs, grated chocolate, and remaining ¼ cup Cognac. Blend all this very firmly with the flour, which you should add a little at a time. When it is perfectly blended, pour over the fruit and nut mixture and mix well with your hands.
7. If bread pans are used, bake the cakes for 1½ hours. If you use a very large springform, the cake should bake about 1 hour longer.
8. Let the fruitcake stand for 1 hour or more after it comes from the oven. Ease the cake out of the pan, carefully peel off paper, and turn top side up to finish cooling. Brush top and sides with Cognac. Wrap in a large piece of Cognac-soaked cheesecloth. Double-wrap in aluminum foil and allow to mature for at least 2 weeks before serving.

YIELD: 30 TO 40 SERVINGS

CAROLE WALTER'S
DARK FRUITCAKE

❧

This dark fruitcake is stuffed with chunks of fruits, including dried apricots, and enriched with thick preserves such as damson plum or a mixture of apricot and pineapple. Dark Jamaican rum is used for soaking the cheesecloth that wraps the cake.

"The chunky fruits absorb the flavorful moisteners, becoming soft and chewy." says Carole Walter. "This recipe can easily be doubled or, if you prefer, halved in four mini-loaves. Make it weeks in advance so the flavor can mature. Then all you need to do is devise pretty wrappings (cellophane is ideal) and you have sensational gifts to offer at holiday time."

1½ cups golden raisins
1 cup pitted dates, cut into ¼-inch pieces
1 cup dried apricots, cut into ¼-inch pieces
1 cup candied pineapple, cut into ¼-inch pieces
2 tablespoons each diced candied lemon rind and orange rind (see Note)
½ cup red and green glacéed cherries, cut into ¼-inch pieces
½ cup currants

1 cup thick preserves (damson plum and apricot/pineapple mixed)
½ cup dark Jamaican rum, plus additional for brushing and for soaking cheesecloth
⅓ cup canned apricot nectar
2¼ cups sifted, unbleached all-purpose flour
1 teaspoon baking soda
¾ teaspoon salt
1½ teaspoons ground cinnamon
¼ teaspoon ground allspice

¼ teaspoon grated nutmeg

¼ teaspoon mace

½ pound (2 sticks) unsalted butter

4 large eggs

1 cup (lightly packed) dark
brown sugar

2 teaspoons vanilla extract

1 cup coarsely hand-chopped pecans

1 cup coarsely hand-chopped
almonds, lightly toasted

2 tablespoons light corn syrup

2 teaspoons hot water

Almond halves and glacéed
cherries for garnish (optional)

1. Combine the raisins, dates, apricots, pineapple, lemon and orange rinds, glacéed cherries, and currants with the preserves, rum, and apricot nectar in a large glass or stainless steel bowl. Cover tightly with plastic wrap or aluminum foil and macerate at room temperature for about 24 hours.

2. Place a large pan on the lowest shelf of the oven and fill with about 1 inch of hot water. Position second rack on the next level up. Preheat the oven to 300 degrees. Butter two 9 x 5 x 2¾-inch loaf pans and line with brown paper.

3. Using a triple sifter, sift together the flour, baking soda, salt, and spices. Set aside.

4. Cut the butter into 1-inch pieces and place them in the large bowl of an electric mixer fitted with beaters or paddle attachment. Soften on low speed. Increase speed to medium-high and cream until smooth and light in color, 1½ to 2 minutes.

5. Reduce mixer speed to low. Gradually add flour mixture over 30 seconds, blending until a stiff batter forms.

6. In the small bowl of an electric mixer, beat the eggs on medium speed for 2 minutes, until thick and light in color. Add the brown sugar, 1 tablespoon at a time, taking 3 to 4 minutes to blend it in well. The mixture should be very thick. Blend in the vanilla. Remove the bowl from the mixer.

7. With a large wooden spoon, stir the egg mixture gradually into the flour batter, blending until smooth. Stir in the hand-chopped nuts and the macerated fruits.

(continued)

8. Spoon the batter into prepared pans, smoothing surface with the back of a tablespoon. Tap pan firmly to remove air pockets. Bake in the preheated oven for 1½ hours.

9. Spoon the corn syrup into a small bowl and mix with the hot water. Five minutes before the end of the baking time, brush the top of each cake with the syrup. If you wish, remove the cake from the oven and gently press halved almonds and glacéed cherries onto the surface. Cover with another thin layer of syrup glaze and bake 5 minutes longer, to set.

10. Cakes are done when they begin to come away from the sides of the pan and a twig of straw or a toothpick inserted into the center comes out clean. Remove from the oven, set the pans on cake racks, and let stand half an hour. Turn the cakes onto their sides and ease them out of the pans. Carefully peel off paper and turn cakes top side up to finish cooling.

11. When cakes are completely cool, brush tops and sides with additional rum. Wrap cakes in large pieces of rum-soaked cheesecloth. You'll need ¼ to ⅓ cup rum for each cake, depending on the size of the piece of cheesecloth. Double-wrap in heavy aluminum foil, sealing well. Allow cakes to mature for at least 2 weeks before serving.

12. Store the wrapped cakes in a cool dry place (a basement is ideal). Remoisten with rum after 2 days and again after 2 weeks. Check again for moistness after 1 month, but remoistening will probably no longer be necessary if cakes were well wrapped. They will keep for up to 6 months. In warm weather, store them in the refrigerator. Serve at room temperature.

YIELD: 12 TO 14 SERVINGS PER LOAF

Note:

If you use candied lemon and orange rinds, reduce the amount of pineapple to ¾ cup.

ROSE LEVY BERANBAUM'S
LESS FRUITY FRUITCAKE

❧

A fruitcake that has more batter than fruit, this one is so moist it can almost be described as a pudding. Molasses provides a slightly bitter edge to take the sweetness off the glacéed fruits. The rum flavor is very subtle.

"Fruitcake is one of the most personal cakes," says Beranbaum. "Either you love it or hate it; prefer all fruit to a more cakelike type; prefer the cake saturated with spirits or the spirits in the background.

"It took years to perfect this recipe because each version had to ripen for three months before tasting and many months would pass between tasting and subsequent re-baking. A taste of this triumphant final fruitcake calls up images of dark Victorian houses filled with secret corners and haunting old memories.

"The texture and flavor of this cake are at their best when the cakes are baked in small pans, which also makes serving the small, rich portions easier. Decorative baking molds such as the Turk's head provide attractive shapes for gift giving."

½ cup small mixed candied fruit
2 tablespoons candied citron
¼ cup dried currants
¼ cup broken pecans
½ cup Myer's dark rum
½ cup unsifted cake flour
¼ teaspoon ground cinnamon
⅛ teaspoon baking soda

¼ teaspoon salt
8 tablespoons (1 stick) unsalted
  butter, softened
¼ cup (firmly packed) dark
  brown sugar
1 large egg
¼ cup unsulfured molasses
2 tablespoons milk

(continued)

1. At least 24 hours before baking the cake, mince the candied fruit and citron (a food processor sprayed lightly with nonstick vegetable spray works beautifully for this sticky task) and soak with the currants and nuts in ¼ cup of the rum. Cover tightly and store at room temperature.
2. Preheat the oven to 325 degrees.
3. Grease and flour a 3½- to 4-cup baking mold or a 6 x 2-inch cake pan. My favorite mold is a 3-cup Turk's head. If using the Turk's head, fill it only three-quarters full and bake the remaining batter in a small greased and floured custard cup.
4. In a small bowl, whisk the flour, cinnamon, baking soda, and salt to combine. In a large mixing bowl, cream the butter and sugar until light and fluffy. Beat in the egg and then the flour mixture in three batches, alternating with the molasses and milk. Add the candied fruit mixture with the soaking rum and beat until blended. The batter will be slightly curdled because of the small amount of flour, but this will not affect the cake's texture.
5. Scrape the batter into the prepared mold and bake 40 to 45 minutes, or until the cake springs back when lightly touched and just begins to shrink from the sides of the pan and a tester comes out clean.
6. Let the cake cool in the pan for 10 minutes and then sprinkle with 2 tablespoons rum. Place a piece of plastic wrap large enough to wrap the cake on the counter. Moisten a piece of cheesecloth also large enough to wrap the cake with 1 tablespoon rum. Place the cheesecloth on the plastic wrap, unmold cake onto it, and sprinkle top with the remaining 1 tablespoon rum. Drape the top and sides of the hot cake with the cheesecloth and plastic wrap, pressing closely to the cake.
7. Let the cake cool to room temperature before covering tightly with heavy-duty foil. Place the cake in an airtight container such as a small tin or heavy-duty

plastic container. If using the tin, run a piece of masking tape around the rim to create a better seal. Keep at cool room temperature for 3 months without opening the container. This will allow the rum to mellow. If you plan to store it longer, unwrap the cake and sprinkle it with an additional tablespoon of rum or else the aromatic edge of the rum will dull and the cake will become dry. Repeat this procedure every 3 months.

YIELD: 10 TO 12 SERVINGS

Variation:

Fruit cupcakes for some mystical reason require no mellowing. They are delicious warm from the oven and remain moist for up to 6 weeks. Fill 8 greased and floured muffin tins three-quarters full and bake at 325 degrees for 20 minutes, or until a cake tester inserted in the center comes out clean. Sprinkle each with 1 teaspoon rum, unmold after 5 minutes, and store airtight at room temperature. For a more decorative shape, use a Bundt-style muffin pan. The batter makes 11 little cakes.

KEN HAEDRICH'S DARK AND MOIST CRANBERRY NUT FRUITCAKE

❧

This cake is particularly moist because it is made with fruit—raisins, cranberries, and dried apricots—that have been cooked in cider. Haedrich also uses dates, precooking them in cider only if he cannot find soft Medjool dates at his local health food store. He also says that dried cherries are excellent in this classic cake for the late fall and early winter months.

1 cup fresh cranberries
1 cup dark raisins
½ cup chopped dried apricots
½ cup apple cider
8 tablespoons (1 stick) unsalted
  butter, softened
½ cup unsulfured molasses
½ cup (packed) light brown sugar
3 large eggs, at room temperature
1 teaspoon vanilla extract
Finely grated peel of 1 orange
2 cups unbleached flour
2 teaspoons baking powder

½ teaspoon baking soda
1 teaspoon salt
1 teaspoon ground ginger
1 teaspoon ground cinnamon
½ teaspoon ground cloves
1 teaspoon unsweetened cocoa
  powder
⅔ cup milk
1 cup chopped pitted dates
1½ cups chopped pecans and
  walnuts
About 1 cup fruit juice (apple,
  cranberry, or orange)

1. Put the cranberries, raisins, apricots, and cider in a medium nonaluminum pot and bring to a boil. Reduce the heat, cover, and cook at a low boil for about 5 minutes. Uncover and cook for another 5 minutes, until the small amount of

remaining liquid is a thick glaze. Scrape the contents of the pot onto a plate and cool to room temperature.

2. Meanwhile, preheat the oven to 350 degrees and butter and flour a 9- or 10-inch tube or kugelhopf pan.

3. With an electric mixer, cream the butter in a large bowl, gradually adding the molasses and brown sugar. Beat in the eggs, one at a time, then the vanilla and the orange peel.

4. Sift the flour, baking powder, baking soda, salt, spices, and cocoa powder into a separate bowl. Stir half the dry mixture into the butter mixture, then fold in the milk, followed by the remaining dry mixture.

5. Once the batter is mixed, fold in the cooked fruit, the dates, and the nuts. Scrape the batter into the prepared pan and bake for about 55 minutes, until a tester inserted in the center comes out clean and the top of the cake feels springy to the touch.

6. Cool the cake in the pan on a rack for 10 minutes, then invert it onto a rack. (If your cake isn't level with the top of the pan, cut a cardboard template and slip it over the tube before you invert the pan. That way you're less likely to break up the cake if it clings to the pan. Simply make a cutout that will fit over the tube and slide down to touch the cake. Then turn the cake over, supporting the cardboard from below. Ease off on the support until the cake drops out.)

7. Cool the cake on the rack—you can leave it on the template if you want—then carefully transfer it to a serving plate. Wrap the cake well to keep it from drying out—the best method is in muslin dipped in fruit juice and wrapped around the cake, followed with plastic and foil. Store the cake in a cool place. Do not keep for more than a week or two, but it is good both freshly baked and later.

YIELD: 16 TO 20 SERVINGS

JULIA CHILD'S FAMOUS STICKY FRUITCAKE

❧

The fruits and nuts for this rich, densely packed cake should macerate overnight. In addition to plentiful quantities of mixed glacéed fruits and nuts, the cake also contains mincemeat, instant coffee, and a mixture of rum with Cognac or bourbon.

"This cake isn't sticky at all, but it started out that way during my first experiment, and the name has remained, as a family joke," says Julia Child. "I decided to work up a very fruity and nutty mixture that was easy to do all alone with no friendly helping hands, and this is it. It's not a budget cake, unfortunately, since a large amount of fruits and nuts can never be an economy affair. But it is so rich and filled with good things that only a small slice should suffice, meaning that one luxury cake can go a long way. It is my habit to make a large amount of anything like this, particularly since it keeps for months and small fruitcakes make wonderful gifts, but you may cut the recipe in half or in thirds if you wish."

THE FRUIT AND NUT MIXTURE (TO BE MACERATED 12 HOURS)

*4 pounds (2 quarts) diced mixed
    glacéed fruits (part of this may
    be diced dried dates, pitted
    and tenderized dried prunes or
    apricots, or raisins or currants)
1 pound (2 cups) store-bought
    prepared mincemeat*

*1 pound (1 quart) mixed
    unsalted whole or chopped nut
    meats (such as walnuts,
    pecans, almonds, cashews,
    filberts)
⅔ cup dark Jamaican rum
⅓ cup Cognac or bourbon*

1 tablespoon instant coffee
(espresso coffee suggested)
1/4 cup dark molasses
1 teaspoon ground cardamom

1/2 teaspoon each: ground
cinnamon, ground cloves,
ground allspice, ground mace
1 1/2 teaspoons salt

THE DRY INGREDIENTS

3 1/2 cups all-purpose flour
(measure by dipping dry-
measure cups into flour and
sweeping off excess)

1 tablespoon double-action
baking powder

THE REMAINING INGREDIENTS

1/2 pound (2 sticks) butter
2 cups white sugar
1/3 cup light brown sugar

2 tablespoons vanilla extract
6 large eggs

OPTIONAL DECORATION AFTER BAKING

1 to 1 1/2 cups Apricot Glaze
(apricot jam pushed through a
sieve, boiled to the thread
stage—228 degrees—with 2
tablespoons sugar per cup of
strained jam)

A dozen or so glacéed cherries
A dozen or so whole pecan or
walnut halves

1. Macerate the fruits and nuts. Turn the glacéed fruits into a very large mixing
bowl, pour on boiling water to cover, stir for 20 to 30 seconds, then drain
thoroughly; this is to wash off any preservatives. Return fruit to bowl, add the

mincemeat, nuts, liquors, instant coffee, molasses, spices, and salt; stir. Cover airtight and let macerate for 12 hours (or longer).

2. Completing the cake mixture. Stir half the flour into the fruits and nuts, sprinkle over the baking powder, and add the rest of the flour, stirring to blend.

3. Using an electric mixer, beat the butter and sugars together in a separate bowl until light and fluffy, then beat in the vanilla and the eggs, one at a time, beating 30 seconds after the addition of each egg. Blend the butter mixture into the fruits.

4. Baking. Preheat the oven to 275 degrees. Butter your cake pan or pans (a 16-inch angel loaf pan or two 9-inch 8-cup pans, or whatever size and combination of pans you wish, including miniature 1-cup loaf pans; you will have a total of 16 cups or more fruitcake batter). Line the bottom with wax paper, butter that, roll flour around in the pan to coat interior, and knock out excess flour. Turn the batter into the pan, filling it to within ¼ inch of rim (mold any extra cake mixture in a muffin tin). Bake in the middle of the oven for 2 to 2¾ hours or longer, depending on the size and shape of pan. The cake will rise about ¼ inch and the top will crack in several places. It is done when it shows the faintest line of shrinkage around edge of pan in several places; a skewer, plunged down into the cake through a crack should come out clean (or, at most, showing a residue of sticky fruit). Remove the cake from the oven and place the pan on a rack to cool for 20 to 25 minutes; the cake should shrink a little more from the sides, showing it is ready to unmold. Turn the cake upside down on rack and give a little shake to unmold it. Peel the paper off bottom and turn the cake carefully right side up—you will need some fancy maneuvering if this is a big cake, like boards for bracing and turning.

5. Additional flavoring. If you wish more Cognac or rum or bourbon flavoring, pour a spoonful or two over the cake two or three times as it cools.

6. When cold, wrap the cake in plastic, then in foil, and store in a cool place. It will keep for months and the flavor matures with age, although the cake makes delicious eating when it is still warm from the oven.

7. If you wish to make a luxurious spectacle of this cake, first paint the top and sides with apricot glaze (be sure the glaze really has boiled to the thread stage so it will not remain sticky when cool). Press halved glacéed cherries and nut meats into the glaze and, for a loaf cake, make a line of cherries down the center, flanked on either side by nut meats. Paint a second coating of glaze over the fruits and the top of the cake. Let set for half an hour at least, allowing the glaze to dry and lose its stickiness. (Although you can still store the cake after glazing, I usually glaze it the day I serve it.)

YIELD: 32 SERVINGS

Fruitcakes containing alcohol can be kept almost indefinitely. Indeed, I read of one family, profiled in *People* magazine in 1987, who had fruitcake that was 109 years old. It was hard as a rock, the article said, and it smelled like moldy rum. The cake was baked late in 1878 by Fidelia Ford, a housewife in Ohio, who set it aside for the following Thanksgiving. She died before the holiday and the family had not the heart to eat the cake without her. They felt the same way the next year, and the next. The cake is now owned by Fidelia's descendants, Morgan Ford and his wife, Dorothy. It resides in a glass compote dish in a china cabinet in their house in Tecumseh, Michigan. In 1966 Morgan's Uncle Amos, who was 86 at the time, tried a piece. He never told anyone what it tasted like.

EDNA LEWIS'S CHRISTMAS FRUITCAKE

❧

This fruitcake contains red wine, brandy, and sorghum molasses. It can be eaten right away or aged for three months.

"When I was a girl, preparations for Christmas started in early September when we children gathered black walnuts, hickory nuts, and hazelnuts. Hazelnuts grew along the edge of the woods on low bushes, but hickories and black walnuts grew on tall trees, and so we had to wait until they fell to the ground before racing with the squirrels to collect them. The black walnuts and hickory nuts were gathered early in autumn to give them time to dry out in the sun: If they were not dry, it was almost impossible to crack their tough inner shells. We'd wedge an upturned flatiron between our knees, put a dried nut on the hard surface, and take a hammer to it. Using a nut pick or sometimes a hairpin we'd pry the nut meats from the shell—rich, flavorful nut meats that even on those warm, bright days, filled us with happy anticipation because we knew they would be baked into Christmas cakes and cookies.

"Whenever there was a break in the harvest, Mother would set about making her fruitcake. It was a family affair that my older sister and I cheerfully participated in. Outside it might be rainy and blowing, but in the snug kitchen the sweet smells of dried fruit, grated fresh nutmeg, and spices kept us warm and happy. Mother bought the dried fruit from the store, and the citron, candied lemon and orange peel, and seedless raisins seemed wonderfully exotic. We took turns chopping quantities of sticky fruit, which we put in a big bowl and macerated in wine and brandy. The batter for the cake was so heavy we had to spell each other during stirring or lay an extra hand on the sturdy wooden spoon. Finally the cake was mixed. Mother spooned the batter into the prepared pans and let it sit overnight to mellow. The next day, whether it was still raining or not, Mother baked the cakes. When they had cooled completely, she wrapped them, still encased in the brown paper that lined the pans, in cheesecloth and put them in a large crock or lard can to age during the months before Christmas.

"Because most everybody cooked with lard in those days, ten-gallon lard cans with wide mouths were common in every household. One cake was set on the bottom of the can, and a partition made of several slats of wood was propped over it so that a second cake could fit on that. Every few weeks we lifted the cakes from the can and sprinkled them with a glassful of brandy, wine, or whiskey to keep them moist and flavorful. Come Christmas, we unwrapped the cakes, sliced one to give away, and put the other on the sideboard to be enjoyed by family and guests during the coming week."

1 cup diced (¼ inch) glazed candied orange peel
1 cup diced (½ inch) glazed candied lemon peel
2 cups ½-inch-long thin strips of citron
1 cup dried currants
2 cups raisins, chopped
½ cup dry red wine
½ cup brandy
3½ cups unbleached all-purpose flour
1 teaspoon ground cinnamon

2 teaspoons grated nutmeg
½ teaspoon ground cloves
1 teaspoon ground allspice
½ teaspoon ground mace
1 teaspoon double-acting baking powder
½ teaspoon salt
½ pound plus 6 tablespoons (2¾ sticks) unsalted butter, softened
2 cups (firmly packed) light brown sugar

*5 large eggs, separated, the whites
at room temperature*
*½ cup sorghum (available at
natural food stores and from
Early's Honey Stand, Route 2,
Spring Hill, Tennessee 37174,
615-486-2230)*

*Brandy, wine, or whiskey for
soaking the cake, if desired*

1. In a large bowl, stir together the orange peel, lemon peel, citron, currants, and raisins. Add the wine and brandy and combine the mixture well. Let fruit macerate, covered, for at least several hours, or overnight.
2. Butter a 10 x 4-inch tube pan (or 2 loaf pans, each 9 x 5 x 3 inches) and line it with parchment paper. To line the tube pan, cut out a 10-inch round of the parchment paper, fold the round in half, and cut out a half circle in the center to fit on the bottom of the tube pan. Cut out a 30 x 4½-inch strip of the parchment paper and fit it around the sides of the pan, cutting the strip, if necessary, to prevent buckling. Cut out a 6½ x 4-inch piece of paper to encircle the tube of the pan. Butter the parchment paper well.
3. Into a bowl, sift the flour twice with the cinnamon, nutmeg, cloves, allspice, and mace. Add the baking powder and salt and sift the mixture again.
4. In the large bowl of an electric mixer, cream the butter with the brown sugar until the mixture is light and fluffy. Add the yolks, beaten lightly, and beat the mixture well. Add the flour mixture, a little at a time, beating well after each addition. Add the sorghum and beat the mixture well. Stir in the fruit mixture with the liquid and combine the mixture well.
5. In a large bowl with a mixer, beat the whites until they just hold stiff peaks. Fold the whites gently but thoroughly into the batter. Spoon the batter into the

prepared pan and let it stand, covered loosely with a kitchen towel, in a cool place overnight to let the flavors mellow.

6. Preheat the oven to 250 degrees.

7. Bake the fruitcake in the middle of the oven for 1 hour and 30 minutes. Remove and cover it with a round of parchment paper with a hole cut in the center to fit around the tube (do not use foil) and bake it for an additional 2 to 2½ hours, or until a tester inserted in the center comes out clean.

8. Let the cake cool completely in the pan on a rack and turn it out onto a work surface, leaving the parchment paper on the cake. Wrap the cake in foil, pack it in a tin, and punch a few holes in the lid or set the lid on loosely. Store the tin in a cool place. Every 2 or 3 weeks up until Christmas, sprinkle the cake with about ½ cup brandy, wine, or whiskey. (The liquor keeps the cake moist and flavorful and helps to preserve it as well.)

YIELD: ABOUT 20 SERVINGS

A shopping poll of 1,000 customers nationwide conducted in 1992 by MasterCard revealed that only 9 percent said they would be giving fruitcake that year. When the poll queried respondents about what they thought was the most appropriate use for a fruitcake, the most popular answer (38 percent) was "a gift for someone else." While 28 percent replied that they would eat it if it appeared in their Christmas stockings, other suggestions for its use included "a good doorstop" (13 percent), "birdfeed" (17 percent), and "landfill" (4 percent).

BERNADETTE'S CARIBBEAN BLACK FRUITCAKE

છ

In the Caribbean, black cake—so named because of its dark color—is served at Christmastime, for birthdays, and at weddings. This cake comes from Henry Thomas and his wife, Denise Svatos, who sell the cakes by mail from New Jersey. They adapted the recipe from Bernadette Taylor, a native of Grenada. They use fruits that have been soaked in rum or port for as long as a year and grind them through a meat grinder before mixing them with the other ingredients. The cakes can be ordered by calling 1-800-533-8837.

3 cups (1 pound) dark raisins
3 cups (1 pound) currants
3 cups (1 pound) pitted prunes
2½ cups glacéed cherries
2 cups mixed candied orange and
lemon peel
1 quart white rum
2 cups (1 pound) firmly packed
dark brown sugar
1 pound (4 sticks) unsalted butter,
plus butter for greasing pans

12 eggs
¼ teaspoon ground cinnamon
¼ teaspoon grated nutmeg
4 cups (1 pound) flour, plus flour
for dusting pans
3 teaspoons baking powder
6 tablespoons burnt sugar
(available in West Indian or
Spanish markets), or substitute
¾ cup gravy coloring
1 quart tawny port

1. Place fruits in a large plastic or glass bowl (not metal). Add 1 cup of the rum. Put through a meat grinder, using a medium blade. Mix with remaining rum so

(continued)

that the ground fruit forms a smooth paste. Cover tightly and let stand in a cool place for at least 2 weeks, or as long as a year.

2. Preheat the oven to 300 degrees. Grease and lightly flour two 10-inch springform baking pans that are at least 3 inches deep.

3. Cream the dark brown sugar and butter. In a separate bowl, combine eggs and spices and whip until foamy. Combine eggs with butter-sugar mixture. Add ground fruits. Mix well. In a separate bowl, mix flour with baking powder. Stir flour mixture into fruit mixture. Add burnt sugar or gravy coloring. Batter should be dark brown.

4. Fill the prepared pans with mixture and bake for 2 hours, or until a tester comes out clean.

5. Take pans out of oven and let cakes cool completely. Pour 1 cup of the port over the top of each. Let it absorb. After 10 minutes, pour on remaining port. Wrap tightly in plastic wrap. (Do not use foil; it will disintegrate.) Let cakes age at least 1 week—the longer the better. Do not refrigerate. Make sure cakes remain moist. If they become dry, moisten with port. The cake can be frozen. Serve with wine, champagne, or port.

YIELD: 30 TO 40 SERVINGS

FLOURLESS FRUITCAKE

❧

This is an extremely rich, dense cake that oddly enough contains neither flour nor sugar. This is not to suggest it contains no calories, however; they are amply provided by the dried fruits. It should be aged at least a month before being served.

½ cup dried apricots
6 slices dried peaches
8 dried figs, chopped
½ cup chopped pitted prunes
1 cup pitted and chopped dates
¾ cup raisins
½ cup dried cherries
½ cup dried cranberries
½ cup chopped candied pineapple
⅔ cup chopped walnuts
⅔ cup blanched and chopped
    almonds
1 cup graham cracker crumbs

½ teaspoon double-acting baking
    powder
¼ teaspoon baking soda
¼ teaspoon salt
½ teaspoon ground cinnamon
¼ teaspoon grated nutmeg
8 tablespoons (1 stick) unsalted
    butter
3 large eggs
⅓ cup honey
½ teaspoon vanilla extract
½ cup brandy

1. Put the apricots and peaches in a large bowl and cover with boiling water. Leave them until they become soft, about 15 minutes.

2. Meanwhile, combine the figs, prunes, dates, raisins, cherries, cranberries, pineapple, walnuts, and almonds in a large bowl. In a small bowl, combine the graham cracker crumbs, baking powder, baking soda, salt, cinnamon, and nutmeg. Mix thoroughly and add to the fruits.

(continued)

3. Remove the apricots and peaches from their soaking water and chop them. Add them to the fruit and reserve the soaking water.
4. Butter a 9 x 5-inch loaf pan and line it with wax paper. Butter the paper. Preheat the oven to 300 degrees.
5. Cream the butter in a food processor or the bowl of an electric mixer. Add the eggs, one at a time, and beat until light and fluffy. Add the honey, vanilla, and brandy and stir into the fruit mixture.
6. Pour the batter into the prepared pan and bake for 1½ to 2 hours, or until a cake tester inserted in the center comes out clean. Let the cake cool in the pan. Turn out of the pan, peel the paper off carefully, and allow the cake to cool completely. Wrap and store in an airtight container for at least a month before serving.

YIELD: ABOUT 12 SERVINGS

Fruitcakes have been prized over the centuries in large part because dried fruit has an edge of luxury to it. It makes sense when you think of a country like England having available some of these fruits year-round in a dried form. Originally cakes containing dried fruits were called "plum cakes," plum being the generic word for dried fruits until the eighteenth century. I believe that fruitcakes are descendants of plum and other puddings, the cake tins being outgrowths of other cooking vessels such as animal bladders and stomachs.

Lorna J. Sass

Pentagon Fruitcake

Since 1986 the following recipe has been used by the Pentagon for a fruitcake that is sent to American servicemen and women at Christmastime.

COMMERCIAL ITEM DESCRIPTION

FRUITCAKE, FRESH

Salient characteristics
Shape—Rectangular, with slightly arched top
Weight—1, 2, 3, or 4 pounds, as specified

FRUITCAKE SHALL BE MADE FROM:

FRUIT AND NUT MIXTURE	PARTS BY WEIGHT
Raisins, golden, seedless	12
Candied cherries (non-running dye)	12
Candied pineapple, natural	25
Candied pineapple, green	20
Candied orange peel, lemon peel, and citron cubes	6
Nutmeat (small pieces of pecans, walnuts, and almonds)	25

Shortening—partially hydrogenated, deodorized shortening shall be free from objectionable odors and flavors. The shortening may contain antioxidants. Butter or margarine may be added for flavor.

Mold inhibitors of proper levels and any other necessary ingredients as allowed by the Federal Food, Drug, and Cosmetic Act.

FINISHED FRUITCAKE:

ஐ Shall not fall apart when sliced.
ஐ Shall not be soft or gummy in center.
ஐ Shall be free from undesirable odors and flavors such as scorched, caramelized, metallic, rancid, or musty.
ஐ Fruits and nuts shall be uniformly distributed throughout.
ஐ Grains shall be uniform.
ஐ Ratio of fruit and nut mixture to cake shall be 70/30.

THE SILVER PALATE'S
NUTTY-AS-A-FRUITCAKE
FRUITCAKE

પ્ર

This is a cake for serious fruitcake lovers. It is packed with dates and walnuts, a sprinkling of candied cherries for color, and just enough "cake" to hold it all together. It is great with afternoon tea at any time of year.

8 cups pitted whole dates
8 cups walnut halves
1 cup glacéed cherries
½ cup unbleached all-purpose
    flour
6 eggs, separated, at room
    temperature
¾ cup granulated sugar
¾ cup (packed) dark brown sugar

6 tablespoons (¾ stick) unsalted
    butter, melted
4½ tablespoons heavy or whipping
    cream
2 tablespoons vanilla extract
2 teaspoons grated orange peel
½ teaspoon almond extract
1½ cups whole wheat flour
1½ teaspoons baking powder

1. Preheat the oven to 325 degrees. Butter three 9 x 5 x 3-inch loaf pans. Line the bottoms and sides with aluminum foil and butter the foil generously.
2. Combine the dates, walnuts, and cherries in a very large bowl or roasting pan. Sprinkle with the all-purpose flour and toss to coat well, separating the dates with your fingers.
3. Combine the egg yolks and both sugars in a large mixing bowl; beat until light and fluffy. Beat in the butter, cream, vanilla, orange peel, and almond extract.

Mix the whole wheat flour and baking powder thoroughly in a small bowl; stir this into the batter with a wooden spoon.

4. Beat the egg whites in another large bowl just until they form stiff peaks. Fold a quarter of the whites into the batter, and then fold in the remaining whites. Pour the batter over the fruit mixture and mix well to coat all the fruit and nuts. Spoon it into the prepared pans, mounding the batter slightly in the pans.

5. Cover the pans with buttered aluminum foil and bake for 40 minutes. Remove the foil from the tops and continue baking until the centers are firm to the touch, 15 to 20 minutes.

6. Cool the cakes in the pans on wire racks. Then remove them from the pans and wrap tightly in aluminum foil. The fruitcake can be eaten the next day or stored in a cool place for up to 2 weeks.

YIELD: ABOUT 25 SERVINGS

JIMMY SCHMIDT'S
AUTUMN HARVEST AND BOURBON
FRUITCAKE

❧

Jimmy Schmidt is chef and owner of the Rattlesnake Club and Très Vite in Detroit, Michigan, and author of *Cooking for All Seasons*. His fruitcake reflects the bounty of a Michigan harvest with its native berries, fruits, and nuts. It is great fresh as well as aged.

Cut the cake carefully with a serrated knife, using a steady sawing action for even slices. It is supple enough to be enjoyed warm with a dollop of spiced whipped cream. It can also be cured in a fresh parchment-lined pan with a good soaking of bourbon, then entirely encased in plastic wrap and stored for several weeks to develop. Repeat the "inoculation" of bourbon every two weeks to help the wonderful cure along, then encase in plastic wrap again.

1 cup golden raisins
1 cup dried pitted cherries
2 cups dried blueberries
1 cup dried cranberries
3 cups Makers Mark bourbon
*　whiskey*
½ pound (2 sticks) unsalted butter
1 to 1½ cups maple sugar
1 to 1½ cups light brown sugar
6 eggs, separated
2 tablespoons vanilla extract
4 cups cake flour

4 teaspoons baking powder
1 cup pumpkin purée (see Note)
1 to 1½ cups large black walnut
*　pieces*
1½ large butternut squash, peeled,
*　quartered, seeded, and cut into*
*　1-inch pieces*
2 teaspoons grated nutmeg
2 teaspoons ground cinnamon
1 teaspoon hot New Mexican
*　chile powder or Hungarian*
*　paprika*

1. In a medium saucepan, combine the dried fruits and the bourbon. Carefully warm the mixture over medium heat until just scalding; do not boil. Remove from heat and allow the fruit to soften in the bourbon, stirring occasionally, for about 1 hour. Transfer into a strainer to drain, collecting the juices, for about 30 minutes.

2. Preheat the oven to 300 degrees. Line two 4 x 9 x 4-inch deep stainless steel loaf pans with buttered parchment paper. Set aside.

3. In a mixing bowl, cream the butter until light. Add both sugars and mix until smooth. Whip in the egg yolks and vanilla.

4. Combine 3 cups of the flour and the baking powder. Slowly add the flour to the creamed butter mixture, alternating additions of the pumpkin purée and juice from the fruit, until all is smoothly combined.

5. In another bowl, combine the fruit, nuts, squash, and spices. Add the remaining 1 cup flour and mix well to coat the fruit. (This step helps keep the fruit and nuts evenly dispersed through the batter.) Add the fruit and nut mixture and mix until just combined.

6. Whip the egg whites to soft peaks. Fold one third of the egg whites into the batter to lighten it. Repeat with the remaining egg whites. Spoon the batter into the buttered and parchment-lined pans. Bake on the lower rack of the oven 1½ to 1¾ hours. The cake is done when it has begun to pull away from the sides of the pan and a tester inserted comes out clean.

7. Remove the cakes to a rack to cool. Turn the cakes out of the pans after 30 minutes, invert on the rack, and allow them to cool completely.

YIELD: ABOUT 24 SERVINGS

Note:

To make pumpkin purée, roast fresh pumpkin for an hour at 375 degrees. One pound of raw pumpkin yields about 1 cup purée.

SUSAN PURDY'S
APRICOT-NUT FRUITCAKE

∾

Unfortunately, many of us shy away from fruitcakes because of overexposure to sickeningly sweet supermarket glacéed fruits. A homemade fruitcake made with the best-quality ingredients bears no resemblance to the store-bought variety; if you make the cake yourself, you can use only those ingredients you prefer. Susan Purdy suggests dried peaches, mangoes, papaya, apples, pineapple, apricots, figs, pears, dates, and prunes in place of candied citron and cherries.

"This is the fruitcake for those who hate candied fruits. A moderately sweet cake containing chopped apricots, three types of nuts, two types of raisins, and grated fresh apples, it is wonderful to give as a gift or to serve for the holidays. It is my personal favorite in the fruitcake department."

2 cups broken walnuts
1 cup hazelnuts or filberts, toasted, skinned, halved or coarsely chopped
1 cup coarsely chopped Brazil nuts or halved pecans
1 cup seedless raisins
1½ cups firmly packed golden raisins
1½ cups firmly packed dried apricot halves, cut into quarters

¾ cup dark rum or Calvados plus ½ cup unsweetened apple cider, or use all spirits
1½ cups unsifted whole wheat pastry flour
2 cups unsifted all-purpose flour
1½ teaspoons baking powder
¼ teaspoon baking soda
½ teaspoon salt
1 teaspoon each ground cinnamon and nutmeg

1½ cups lightly salted butter (3
   sticks), at room temperature,
   or use ½ cup margarine plus 1
   cup butter
1½ cups firmly packed light
   brown sugar
5 large eggs
2 teaspoons vanilla extract

1 cup unpeeled grated apple,
   cooking type such as Granny
   Smith (6 ounces)
1 cup applesauce
Apricot Glaze (page 53)
Walnut, almond, or pecan halves,
   or cut-up dried apricots for
   garnish

1. A day or two before baking the cake, combine all the dried fruits and nuts in a large bowl and toss well with the rum or Calvados, and cider. Cover with plastic wrap and set aside in a cool place for at least 24 hours. Toss the mixture occasionally.

2. On the baking day, prepare the pans. Lightly grease them and cut paper liners to cover both bottom and sides. Press the paper in place, then grease the paper. Position the rack in the center of the oven for 1 large cake, or divide the oven in thirds for several cakes. Preheat the oven to 325 degrees.

3. Sift both flours, the baking powder, baking soda, salt, and spices together onto wax paper. Set aside. Use a spoon and a mixing bowl or an electric mixer to cream together the butter and sugar until well blended. Add the eggs one at a time, beating after each addition. Stir in the vanilla extract.

4. Add the flour mixture in three or four additions, beating very slowly to blend after each addition. The batter will be quite stiff. Stir in the grated apple and applesauce. Stir the macerated fruit-nut-rum mixture, then add it to the batter along with all the liquid. Stir the batter with a sturdy wooden spoon until well blended; the best way to blend is with your bare hands.

5. Spoon the batter into the prepared pan(s), filling them about two-thirds full. Bake in the preheated oven for 1½ to 1¾ hours for a 9- or 10-inch tube cake, or

about 1 hour and 15 minutes for baby loaves. A cake is done when the top is golden brown (cracking is normal as the steam escapes) and a cake tester inserted in the center shows no visible raw batter.

6. Cool each cake on a wire rack for 20 minutes. Run a knife blade around the cake sides to loosen, then top with a cardboard cake disk or plate and invert; remove the pan and peel off the paper. Invert again and cool the cake completely right side up. Once cold, the cakes may be served or stored. Store them wrapped in plastic wrap, then foil, in the refrigerator for about 2 weeks for the flavors to mellow, then serve or freeze them. Of course, it is also fine to eat this cake right after baking. Do not wrap it with alcohol-soaked cloths for storage.

7. Before serving, brush the cake with Apricot Glaze and set a few halved nuts and cut pieces of apricot into the soft glaze. Allow about 30 minutes for the glaze to set.

YIELD: 12 TO 14 SERVINGS

You need to cultivate a taste for fruitcake. But be warned, it has more calories than anything else.

Marion Cunningham

APRICOT GLAZE

❧

This makes a very attractive glaze for fruitcakes. Nuts and glacéed fruits can be pressed into it for a dramatic effect.

2 cups apricot jam   *2 tablespoons water*

1. Put the jam and the water into a small saucepan. Simmer gently for 2 to 3 minutes, making sure it does not stick to the bottom of the pan (add more water if necessary).
2. Push the jam through a strainer. While the glaze is still warm, apply it to the cake with a pastry brush. For fruitcakes, a thin glaze is preferable. If this glaze gets too thick, add a teaspoon of hot water.

YIELD: ENOUGH FOR TWO 10-INCH CAKES

MARION CUNNINGHAM'S CHOCOLATE FRUITCAKE

eɔ

Chocolate fruitcakes sound particularly decadent, and they are delicious. Chocolate goes very well with unsweetened dried fruits—and with brandy. This combination of chocolate, cinnamon, and brandy is unusual and very good.

⅓ cup raisins
2 tablespoons brandy
2 ounces unsweetened chocolate
8 tablespoons (1 stick) unsalted
    butter, or ½ cup shortening
1¼ cups sugar
2 eggs
1 teaspoon vanilla extract

1 cup milk
2 cups cake flour
2 teaspoons baking powder
½ teaspoon salt
2 teaspoons ground cinnamon
⅓ cup candied cherries
½ cup chopped walnuts

1. Soak the raisins in the brandy for at least 2 hours, or overnight if possible.
2. Melt the chocolate in a pot or bowl over simmering water; set aside to cool.
3. Preheat the oven to 350 degrees. Butter and lightly flour two 8-inch round cake pans.
4. Cream the butter or shortening in a large mixing bowl. Gradually add the sugar and beat until light. Add the eggs and beat well. Beat in the chocolate and the vanilla, then add the milk and beat well.
5. Mix together the flour, baking powder, salt, and cinnamon and add to the batter, beating thoroughly. Stir in the raisins and brandy, cherries, and walnuts.
6. Spread the batter in the pans and bake for about 35 minutes, testing until a toothpick comes out clean. Cool in the pans for 5 minutes before turning out onto a rack.

YIELD: ABOUT 16 SERVINGS

CHRISTOPHER IDONE'S FRUITCAKE
WITH APRICOT-BOURBON SAUCE

❧

Christopher Idone, chef and author of several cookbooks including *Glorious Food* and *Glorious American Food*, was a cofounder of the New York catering firm called Glorious Foods. The cake gets its rich, dark color from espresso coffee, melted bitter chocolate, and a long period of aging. Just before serving it, Idone brushes the cake with a warm apricot-bourbon sauce.

"Christmas isn't Christmas without fruitcake. For years I have given them as presents. People either said, that's the best fruitcake I've ever had, or they muttered something about having given the cake to someone else. For people either love or hate them. We came up with our fruitcake, which is packed with fruits and nuts, after years of adding and subtracting a variety of ingredients. To make this truly delicious cake, douse it every so often with Cognac, so that it is completely 'inebriated' before being brought to the table. You might wish to steam it, as you would a Christmas pudding and serve it flamed in a Cognac bath. (In the South, fruitcakes are often doused with corn whiskey instead of Cognac. It's a nice change.)"

*1 pound (4 sticks) unsalted
 butter, at room temperature
2⅔ cups (firmly packed) dark
 brown sugar (soft, not
 granular)
12 large eggs*

*4 cups sifted all-purpose flour
1 teaspoon ground cinnamon
¾ teaspoon ground mace
⅛ teaspoon ground cloves
½ teaspoon baking soda
2 ounces bitter chocolate*

½ cup strong espresso, chilled
6 cups (2 pounds) raisins
2½ cups (1 pound) candied red
cherries
6 cups (1½ pounds) currants
2 cups (½ pound) sultana raisins
1½ cups (½ pound) citron, grated
1½ cups (½ pound) candied
orange peel, chopped fine
1½ cups (½ pound) candied
lemon peel, chopped fine

1½ cups (½ pound) candied
pineapple, cut into eighths
2½ cups (1½ pounds) whole
hazelnuts
2 cups (1½ pound) walnut pieces
1 cup unsifted all-purpose flour to
dust the fruit
Unsalted butter for the brown
paper
Cognac, bourbon, or corn whiskey
for aging

For the Apricot Sauce

1 cup apricot jam

2 ounces bourbon

1. Using an electric mixer, cream the butter until it is light and fluffy. Add the sugar and blend thoroughly. Add the eggs, one at a time, and mix them in thoroughly. Fold in the flour, spices, and baking soda and blend thoroughly.
2. Melt the chocolate over simmering water in the top of a double boiler; remove from the heat and let cool. Fold the chocolate and coffee into the batter (this will loosen the batter and give it a rich color as well). Set aside.
3. In an extra-large bowl, combine the fruit and nuts, dust with the flour, and toss to mix. Pour in the batter and mix thoroughly.
4. Preheat the oven to 275 degrees. Line six 2½-cup fancy molds (fluted tube pans) with buttered brown paper. (Cut the buttered paper into blunted triangles to fit.) You may also use two 8 x 2-inch round pans or a 9 x 5 x 3-inch loaf pan.
5. Fill the molds in pans to within ½ inch of the tops with the batter mixture. Bake for 1 hour and 45 minutes to 2 hours, or until a kitchen needle comes out clean.

(continued)

6. Sprinkle the cakes with the liquor and allow them to cool in the oven with the oven door slightly ajar.
7. When cool, unmold the cakes, leaving them wrapped in the paper. Wrap the cakes in cheesecloth, then in foil. Place the cakes in plastic bags or airtight containers. Unwrap and douse the cakes with liquor every 7 to 10 days for at least 6 weeks.
8. When you are ready to serve the cakes, make the apricot sauce. In a heavy saucepan, bring the jam and bourbon to a boil over medium heat. When the sauce begins to boil, remove from the heat and strain. Brush the cakes with the hot apricot sauce.

YIELD: ABOUT 30 SERVINGS

JUDY ROSENBERG'S
CHOCOLATE FRUITCAKE

ℰℛ

This is a dense cake aged in liquor, but the chocolate and unsweetened dried fruits make it stand out. The cake gets better as it ages.

2 cups chopped mixed dried fruits,
such as apricots, dates, prunes,
pears, and raisins
6 tablespoons Grand Marnier or
other orange liqueur
2 tablespoons Cognac
3 ounces unsweetened chocolate
½ cup plus 1 tablespoon all-
purpose flour

½ teaspoon baking powder
8 tablespoons (1 stick) unsalted
butter, at room temperature
1 cup sugar
3 large eggs, at room temperature
½ cup chopped walnuts, almonds,
or pecans
¼ cup Cognac for brushing the
cake

1. Combine the dried fruits, Grand Marnier, and Cognac in a small bowl or container and allow it to sit, covered, for 24 hours. Toss the fruits occasionally to ensure they are completely saturated.
2. The next day, melt the chocolate in the top of a double boiler placed over simmering water. Let it cool.
3. Preheat the oven to 325 degrees. Line a 9½ x 5½ x 2-inch baking pan with a piece of greased wax paper that overhangs both long sides of the pan by 2 inches.
4. Sift together the flour and baking powder in a small bowl and set aside.
5. Beat the butter and sugar in a medium-size mixing bowl with an electric mixer on medium speed until light and fluffy, about 2 minutes.

(continued)

6. Add the chocolate to the butter mixture and beat on medium speed until completely blended, about 10 seconds. Scrape the bowl with a rubber spatula.

7. Add the eggs, one at a time, and mix on low speed after each addition for 10 seconds. Scrape the bowl each time. Increase the speed to medium and mix 15 seconds longer.

8. Add the flour mixture and mix on low speed just until blended, about 8 seconds. Scrape the bowl.

9. Stir in the fruit (and any remaining liquid) and the nuts by hand with a wooden spoon.

10. Spoon the batter into the prepared pan. Bake on the center oven rack until a tester inserted in the center comes out with a moist crumb, 1 to 1¼ hours.

11. Allow the cake to cool in the pan before removing it. Remove the paper.

12. Brush some of the Cognac over all surfaces of the cake. Wrap the cake in cheesecloth or a light cotton cloth and brush the cloth with the Cognac.

13. Place the cake in a container or Ziploc bag and refrigerate it. If you plan to keep it for several weeks or months, brush it with more Cognac when the cloth is dry.

YIELD: 12 TO 14 SERVINGS

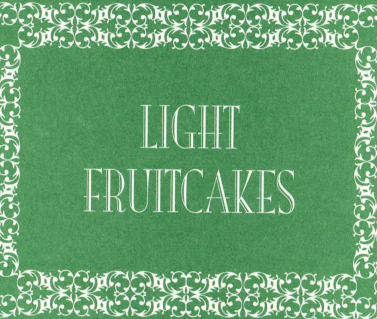

LIGHT
FRUITCAKES

Many of the recipes in this chapter come from the South, where fruitcake has always been extremely popular. In the nineteenth century, hundreds of fruitcake recipes were routinely printed and passed around the community. According to the late Bill Neal, they usually contained a combination of citron, almond, coconut, and occasionally a few currants. Only later were ingredients such as bourbon, pecans, and glacéed cherries added. An especially popular Southern dessert from the Edwardian era is Japanese fruitcake, which has a rich fruit and nut filling and is coated with fluffy white icing flavored with coconut.

At the other end of the scale is Jeff Smith's fruitcake, which is not nearly so rich, being made with applesauce. Ken Haedrich's unusual cake contains ricotta cheese and whole wheat flour, along with dried coconut and dark rum.

These are more subtle and delicate, and less rich than the robust dark fruitcakes. Most have a rich yellow pound cake base laced with candied fruits—green and red cherries, pineapple, walnuts, raisins—that make a pretty mosaic when the cakes are sliced.

If you keep a light fruitcake for a week or two, its texture becomes more dense. It will keep well wrapped in a tightly sealed container, but most of the cakes in this chapter do not last for months like dark fruitcakes.

SOLID EVIDENCE OF CHRISTMAS

by Robert Farrar Capon

❧

Breathes there a man with tastes so dead who never to himself has said, on having yet another holiday fruitcake delivered to his doorstep, "Whatever happened to the cake in these concoctions?"

[Capon offers the following possible explanation:]

Since the public would be unwilling to purchase fruitcakes of a size large enough to contain all of these ingredients (the usual assortment of dried fruits and nuts)—and since making them smaller (the fruitcakes) would raise the probability that a given fruit or nut might not find its way into a given cake—the purveyors of fruitcakes found themselves forced to choose between the two basic components of their product. The cake, of course, lost, giving rise to the now omnipresent and unavoidable holiday gift: the fruit brick. In recent studies by the physics departments of major universities, the atomic weight of this remarkable confection has been calculated to just below that of uranium.

This extreme density, it was discovered, is due to the method by which modern fruitcakes are made. After the manufacturers abandoned the use of agglutinating agents such as flour and eggs, they developed a special bonding technique by which the fruit and nuts were compacted by a hydraulic press. This special piece of "bakery" equipment, seventy times more powerful than the ram that reduces used cars to crumpled blocks, creates in the "cake" an internal pressure so great that the fruits and nuts adhere to each other by their own molecular attraction.

The New York Times, December 14, 1983

THE SMITH FAMILY FRUITCAKE

by Jeffrey Steingarten

❧

I was eighteen when I first tasted a Christmas fruitcake, which may explain why I liked it so much. My family never celebrated Christmas, except by watching the first fifteen minutes of "Amahl and the Night Visitors" on television, and nothing in my grandmothers' repertory had prepared me for that first wondrous mouthful at the house of a friend from college. It was a moist, alcoholic plum pudding, full of dark, saturated, medieval tastes and colors—currants, dates and black raisins, aromatic orange peel, mace and allspice and nutmeg, brandy and molasses—aged for a year and then set aflame at the very last minute, carefully spooned out like the treasure it was, and topped with an astonishing ivory sauce made simply of butter, sugar, brandy, and nutmeg. That's nothing but hard sauce, it was explained to me. No more belittling name has ever been conferred upon so massive a culinary triumph.

Nowadays mail-order fruitcake companies advertise fruitcakes for people who can't stand fruitcake, which makes no more sense to me than

concocting a new kind of foie gras for people who can't stand foie gras. I've ordered several of them over the years; most are loosely cemented blocks of nuts and hard, dried fruits (no sugar added) with barely any cake in between; one is baked in the shape of the state of Texas. Cookbooks inexplicably offer creative alternatives to hard sauce, and a few years back, Hallmark issued a series of anti-fruitcake greeting cards. I'll bet the most widely published food joke in history is Calvin Trillin's libel that there is just one fruitcake in the world, never eaten but simply passed on from year to year.

Many Christmas customs still puzzle me. Why, for instance, would you want to celebrate a joyous event by going out and killing a pine tree, draping it with shredded aluminum foil and dyed popcorn, and throwing it into the garbage a week later? By now I have eaten as many fruitcakes as any God-fearing Christian and I can't imagine what everybody is complaining about.

Fruitcake entered my life on a permanent basis twenty years ago, when the woman who was to become my wife moved in, bringing with her all the edible mores of a Mormon upbringing (her family abounds with members of the Daughters of Utah pioneers, though an errant grand-uncle once joined the Butch Cassidy gang in Baggs, Wyoming). Every year, right after Thanksgiving, her mother, Marjorie, mailed us several small white fruitcakes neatly wrapped in wax paper and meant to be aged and ripened in the refrigerator until Christmas. We would observe this rule with only one of them and polish off the others, paper-thin slice by paper-thin slice, before December arrived. Two weeks later Aunt Vivian from Salt Lake City would send a large dark, spicy fruitcake suspended in a shoebox with her patented protective caramel-popcorn insulation.

Sometimes the shoebox was large enough to hold another little package filled with delicate sugar cookies decorated with red and green sprinkles. In keeping with Mormon religious rules, none of the family's fruitcakes contained any alcohol.

Marjorie Smith's white fruitcake quickly became my favorite. The recipe was sent to us by Aunt Esther in Twin Falls, but Esther never sent us any fruitcake and Marjorie never failed to, which is why I always think of it as Marjorie's. It is, at bottom, a rich, yellow lemon pound cake, unleavened, slightly underbaked, and filled with a volume of fruit and nuts equal to that of cake batter—green and red candied cherries and pineapple, walnuts, and yellow raisins.

The other day I was thumbing through ten year's worth of women's magazines—looking in vain for good advice about making and mailing edible Christmas gifts and discovering instead a recipe for chocolate-chip pretzel bread—and I came across several warnings not to use popcorn or cereal as the filler in your Christmas package. They are thought to entice insects and absorb noxious fumes. But let me assure you that the candied popcorn protecting Aunt Vivian's fruitcake never attracted the tiniest insect or the merest wisp of a noxious fume. The magazines suggest using crumpled newspaper instead. That works fine if you mail your gift from Salt Lake City and crumple up a copy of *Deseret News,* but if you live in New York or Los Angeles, your lucky recipient is likely to read "Store Santa Slashes Tots, Self, on Sleigh" before he or she reaches the delicacies within.

When my wife moved in she had twenty-two living aunts and uncles and you never knew whether Aunt Melva would send a box of her taffy or Aunt Frances a jar of her jam cooked from berries she had picked the summer before near her home in Olympic State Forest. Some years Aunt Evelyn in Salt Lake City would send us a tin of her famous butter mints, a delicate, creamy candy arduously made from hand-pulled sugar. At the age of eighty, Evelyn recently supplied butter mints to four hundred guests at her grand-daughter's wedding (two per customer), and once a year she makes them for the twenty-eight widows living in her Ward and put under her charge, but she never sends enough to us. Evelyn also does cookies, including Date Swirl fruitcake light and dark; and Million-Dollar Fudge. Evelyn is one reason Utah is called the Beehive State.

If I detect a competitive or compulsive edge to the food giving of the Salt Lake City area—I once observed two women frantically trying to force platters of fudge on each other as though they contained toxic waste—it is a contest from which the observer can only benefit. But as the years pass and Christmases come and go like clockwork, fewer of my wife's relations are able to bake as much as they would like, and most of the younger generation seem more skilled with the can opener than the canning jar. But Marjorie and Aunt Vivian kept the fruitcakes coming till the end. Five years ago, after an illness, Aunt Vivian substituted what people in Salt Lake City call TV Mix or TV Crunch, which is a mélange of Wheat Chex, Corn Chex, Rice Chex, peanuts, and pretzel sticks tossed with onion salt and soy sauce, and intended, presumably, to be enjoyed while watching television. Trying not to sound ungrateful, we phoned Vivian to let her know how much we missed her fruitcake. The following Christmas she came out of retirement at the age of eighty-eight.

Now Vivian and Marjorie are gone. Last year, as Christmas approached, I finally acknowledged that no matter how many times I ran down to the mailbox, the fruitcakes would never arrive. The idea of baking them myself did not instantly occur to me. Real men do not bake fruitcake.

One night I could stand it no longer. My kitchen was well stocked with flour, butter, eggs, raisins and walnuts, but sadly lacking in the lemon extract and candied fruit department. Unlike Salt Lake City, New York is a twenty-four-hour town, so I hopped in a cab and traveled from one all-night bodega and Korean grocer to another in search of red and green candied cherries and pineapple. By midnight I was desperate. I toyed with the idea of buying thirty boxes of Jujyfruits and removing the licorice ones. But at last some candied fruit miraculously appeared, plastic tubs of bright green and red cherries, sufficient even without the pineapple for my immediate needs, and by two in the morning the fruitcakes were done. I aged one of them for nearly five minutes and cut it open, and it came close enough to Marjorie's white fruitcake to calm me down until the stores opened in the morning. Since then I have baked the cake many times, using Aunt Esther's advice to clear up various ambiguities in the recipe and add some new ones. My wife can't tell it from her mother's.

Once you learn to relate to fruitcake, there is no end to the recipes you can try.

Light Fruitcakes

JEFFREY STEINGARTEN'S
SMITH FAMILY WHITE FRUITCAKE

This recipe from Jeffrey Steingarten's wife's family in Utah makes a rich, yellow pound cake filled with fruit and nuts—green and red candied cherries and pineapple, walnuts, and golden raisins.

"After you keep it in the refrigerator for a week or two, it becomes dense and less cakelike, and when you slice it thin, the result is a translucent, frolicsome mosaic of yellows, reds, and greens, two of which, I believe, are the official colors of Christmas."

2 cups candied red cherries
2⅔ cups mixed green and red
candied pineapple
2⅔ cups yellow raisins
3 cups walnut halves
1 pound (4 sticks) unsalted
butter, at room temperature

2¼ cups granulated white sugar
6 large eggs
4 cups sifted all-purpose flour
3 tablespoons lemon extract

1. Halve the candied cherries and cut the pineapple into half-inch pieces. Put all the candied fruits in a strainer and wash them under cold water. Mix them thoroughly with the raisins and walnuts in a bowl with a 6-quart capacity or more.

2. Preheat the oven to 300 degrees. Butter two 9 x 5 x 4-inch loaf pans and line them with parchment paper or brown paper. Butter the paper. (This recipe makes 16 cups of cake batter, enough for two 8-cup loaf pans. Or you can make

a dozen small fruitcakes in miniature nonstick loaf pans; decrease the baking time accordingly). The Smith family uses brown paper, which they feel prevents the cakes from becoming dark and crusty on the outside, a fatal flaw.

3. In a mixer, beat the butter until it is light, add the sugar, and beat until fluffy. Beat in 3 of the eggs, 2 cups of the flour, the other 3 eggs, and finally the remaining 2 cups of flour. Beat in the lemon extract. Pour the cake batter over the fruit and nuts and thoroughly fold everything together with a large spatula.

4. Pour and scrape the batter into the pans, leaving at least ¼ inch for the cakes to expand. Bake the fruitcakes for 45 minutes, cover tightly with aluminum foil (leaving space above the top of the cake), and bake for another 45 minutes. Do not overbake. These cakes should be slightly underdone and very moist; remove them from the oven as soon as they resist the pressure of your fingertips or show the barest sign of pulling away from the sides of the pan. Let the fruitcakes cool in their pans on a rack, unmold them, and refrigerate for at least a few days and as long as 3 weeks before cutting them into slices while they are still cold.

YIELD: ABOUT 32 SERVINGS

I always enjoy a good fruitcake, however I don't have any particular favorite recipes—I've never made one. I must say that I really like fruitcakes best when they are moist and full of home-candied fruit.

Alice Waters

JEFF SMITH'S GRAM'S LIGHTER
APPLESAUCE FRUITCAKE

༄

For those who prefer lighter fruitcakes, this is an excellent one—and it can be eaten right away.

"As my mother grew older, her tastes changed," says Jeff Smith. "All of us pass through such a thing. Finally, by the grace of God, she stopped making those heavy, dark fruitcakes. This new version is of her new mind, and I like it very much. It is simple to prepare."

1 cup (2 sticks) butter, at room
temperature
2 cups sugar
2 eggs, at room temperature
2 teaspoons vanilla extract
2 cups coarsely chopped pitted
dates
3 cups applesauce
2 cups coarsely chopped walnuts

2 cups raisins
2 cups coarsely chopped mixed
candied fruit
½ teaspoon salt
1 teaspoon ground cinnamon
½ teaspoon ground cloves
1 tablespoon baking soda
4 cups all-purpose flour

1. Preheat the oven to 350 degrees. Grease three 8 x 4 x 3-inch loaf pans with butter.
2. Cream the butter and sugar together. Beat in the eggs, one at a time, along with the vanilla extract. Add the remaining ingredients and blend until all is incorporated.
3. Divide the batter among the 3 greased loaf pans. Bake for 1 hour and 15

minutes, or until the cakes begin to pull away from the sides of the pan and a toothpick inserted in the center comes out clean.

4. Remove to a cooling rack. When cool enough to handle, remove the loaves from the pans and cool completely on the rack. Wrap in plastic and keep in the refrigerator. They will keep about 2 weeks.

YIELD: ABOUT 30 SERVINGS

JOSEPHINE SOKOLOV'S VERY RICH
NO-HOLDS-BARRED FRUITCAKE

෨

Raymond Sokolov's mother has made this cake, which contains a generous amount of Brazil nuts, for the last forty years. Sokolov suggests using Brazil nuts in their shells. If you put them in a low oven on a cookie sheet and leave them until the smell begins to permeate the kitchen (it isn't a very long time), they crack easily—as long as you crack them before they cool. They are slightly toasted and have a definitely improved flavor (they are also much less expensive to buy than shelled Brazil nuts). If you have any left over, Sokolov suggests you make Brazil nut brittle.

"I changed a recipe that I found in a magazine years ago by making it simpler," says Josephine Sokolov. "We don't age the cake, we eat it right away."

3 cups Brazil nuts (1½ pounds after shelling)	¾ cup sugar
2 packages (6½ ounces each) pitted dates	½ teaspoon baking powder
	½ teaspoon salt
1 cup maraschino cherries	3 eggs
¾ cup sifted all-purpose flour	1 teaspoon vanilla extract

1. Preheat the oven to 300 degrees. Grease a 9 x 5 x 3-inch loaf pan and line the bottom and sides with greased wax paper.
2. Put the whole Brazil nuts, whole dates, and whole drained cherries into a large bowl. In a separate bowl, sift together the flour, sugar, baking powder, and salt. Pour the mixture over the fruit and mix thoroughly with your hands.

3. In a separate bowl, beat the eggs until frothy, then add the vanilla. Pour the egg mixture over the fruit mixture and mix with your hands.
4. Pour the mixture into the loaf pan and bake for 1 hour at 300 degrees. Turn the oven up to 325 degrees and bake for 45 minutes longer. Remove from pan, discard the wax paper, and keep the cake tightly wrapped in foil. It will keep about 2 weeks.

YIELD: ABOUT 12 SERVINGS

MAIL-ORDER FRUITCAKES

Some of the best fruitcakes are available by mail from Trappist monks. One that is made in Berryville, Virginia, was described by the late Nika Hazelton as simply wonderful. "It had a world of fruit in it (nothing like the all-too-scant fruit in most commercial cakes), so that greed got the better of me, and I kept stealing back to the cake to sink my teeth into that absolutely heavenly mixture of glacéed fruit and nuts, with everything soused in brandy (and very good brandy too)." It comes from The Monastery, Holy Cross Abbey, Berryville, Virginia 22611.

Another good fruitcake is made by Trappist monks at Gethsemani, where Thomas Merton, author of numerous books, articles, and poems and the most celebrated monk of the twentieth century, lived and worked. The cakes are topped with pecans and cherries and contain, among other (secret) ingredients, fresh orange and lemon rind, strong Italian table wine, and Kentucky bourbon. Aged for ten or eleven months before being sold, the fruitcakes are made from a recipe created in 1955. They can be ordered from Gethsemani Farms, Trappist, Kentucky 40051.

EUDORA WELTY'S
WHITE FRUITCAKE

✑

This recipe was privately printed in a limited edition as a Christmas greeting in 1980. The slices of cake come out rich and translucent. Make the cake several weeks ahead of Christmas if you can.

3 cups (1 pound) clear crystallized pineapple
3 cups (1 pound) glacéed cherries, half green, half red
4 cups (1 pound) pecan halves
4 cups flour, sifted before measuring, plus some for dusting fruit and nuts
¾ pound (3 sticks) unsalted butter

2 cups sugar
2 teaspoons baking powder
Pinch of salt
6 eggs, separated
Citron or lemon peel, if desired
1 teaspoon vanilla extract
Dash of freshy grated nutmeg
1 cup bourbon

1. Prepare the pans—the sort with a chimney or a tube—by greasing them well with Crisco and then lining them carefully with three layers of wax paper, all greased as well.
2. Prepare the fruit and nuts ahead. Cut the pineapple into thin slivers and the cherries in half. Break up the pecan meats, reserving a handful or so of shapely halves to decorate the tops of the cakes. Put in separate bowls, dusting fruit and nuts lightly with siftings of flour, to keep them from clustering together in the batter.
3. In a very large wide mixing bowl (a salad bowl, or even a dishpan will serve), cream the butter very lightly, then beat in the sugar until all is smooth and

creamy. Sift in the flour, with baking powder and salt added, a little at a time, alternating with the unbeaten egg yolks added one at a time.

4. When all this is creamy, add the floured fruit and nuts, gradually scattering them lightly into the batter, stirring all the while, along with the citron, vanilla, and nutmeg. Add the bourbon in alternation, little by little.

5. Lastly, whip the egg whites into peaks and fold in.

6. Set the oven low, about 250 degrees. Pour the batter into the cake pans, remembering that they will rise. Decorate the tops with nuts. Bake for 3 hours or more, until they spring back to the touch and a straw inserted at the center comes out clean and dry. (If the top browns too soon, lay a sheet of foil lightly over.) When done, the cakes should be a warm golden color.

7. When they've cooled enough to handle, run a spatula around the sides of each cake, cover the pan with a big plate, turn the pan over, and slip the cake out. Cover the cake with another plate and turn it right side up. When cool, the cake can be wrapped in cloth or foil and stored in a tightly fitting tin box.

8. From time to time before Christmas, you may improve it with a little more bourbon, dribbled over the top to be absorbed and so ripen the cake before cutting. This cake will keep for a good while, in or out of the refrigerator.

YIELD: ABOUT 30 SERVINGS

JACQUES PÉPIN'S
CHRISTMAS FRUITCAKE

そう

This fruitcake can be made without the mixture of dried and candied fruit to produce a very rich pound cake. However, Pépin says that they greatly enhance the cake and make it a festive holiday dessert. He also cuts the cake into tiny pieces for petits fours.

Pépin candies the peel himself, a simple and inexpensive procedure that results in candied peel that is infinitely superior to the store-bought variety. He says that a mixture of the peels and dried fruits will keep almost indefinitely if covered with rum and stored in a jar in the refrigerator. They can be added to soufflés as well as to cakes and fruit salads.

The cake is baked slowly for a long time, until completely set inside. When cool, it should be wrapped in plastic and stored in an airtight container. It can also be frozen.

FOR THE CANDIED PEELS

1 grapefruit	6 cups cold water
1 tangerine	¾ cup sugar
1 lime	1½ cups water
1 lemon	

FOR THE DRIED FRUIT

½ cup diced dried apricots	⅓ cup raisins
⅓ cup diced dried pears	⅓ cup dark rum
⅓ cup diced dried peaches	

For the Cake Batter

½ pound plus 4 tablespoons (2½ sticks) butter, softened
1 cup sugar
5 eggs

3 tablespoons orange juice
¼ teaspoon salt
2 cups all-purpose flour
½ cup cake flour

1. The candied peels include not only the colored parts of the skin, but also the pith. Cut wedges through grapefruit and other citrus fruits, pull the skin away from the fruit, and cut into ¼-inch dice. (The fruit can be used for juice or in salads). You may also use the peel that is left over after your morning orange or grapefruit juice.

2. Place the diced fruit peels in 3 cups of the cold water, bring to a boil, and cook over high heat for about 1 minute. Drain in a colander and rinse the pieces for a few seconds under cold water. Rinse the saucepan and add the remaining 3 cups of cold water. Repeat the boiling, draining, and rinsing procedure and rinse the saucepan again. (The blanching process removes any bitterness from the peel.) Finally, place the diced peels back in the saucepan with the sugar and 1½ cups water and cook for about 15 minutes, until most of the moisture is reduced to a very syrupy liquid.

3. Combine the diced apricots, pears, peaches, and raisins and add to the candied peels and syrup. Mix in the dark rum. At this point, the mixture can be refrigerated and kept almost indefinitely.

4. Preheat the oven to 350 degrees. Cut a strip of parchment paper long enough to fit the length of a loaf pan and extend 1½ inches beyond it at either end (this makes it easy to unmold the cake after baking). Butter the paper and the bottom and sides of the mold and position the paper in the mold, pressing to make it adhere to the bottom and sides and either end.

5. For the cake batter, combine the butter and sugar in the bowl of a mixer. Add the eggs, orange juice, salt, and both flours and beat with the flat beater just enough to incorporate. Add the candied peels and dried fruit and fold them in gently with a spatula. Pour the batter into the prepared pan and smooth the top with a spatula.

6. Place the loaf pan on a cookie sheet and bake for about 45 minutes. Reduce the heat to 325 degrees and bake for another 60 to 70 minutes, until completely set inside.

7. Allow the cake to cool in the pan. When cool, wrap in plastic wrap and/or aluminum foil and keep either frozen or in the refrigerator. At serving time, cut into ½-inch slices and serve. This cake is a nice accompaniment to cream custard but can also be served alone or with fruit and nuts.

YIELD: 12 SERVINGS

If you can locate a source of candied peel—orange, lemon, or citron sold by the piece (it will resemble halves or quarters of the peel left intact)—by all means use this and dice it yourself, rather than use the diced, packaged variety. If, as a last resort, you must use the standard supermarket variety of diced candied fruit or peel, be sure to rinse it well, chop it fine, and soak it in rum or orange liqueur for a few hours before using it in a dessert.

Nick Malgieri

PAULA PECK'S
WHITE FRUITCAKE WITH PECANS
 భ

This is a particularly light and delicate cake, with the added luxury of pecans.

The batter should be folded gently, just enough to combine the ingredients without overmixing so that the cake does not become heavy.

2 cups mixed, diced candied fruit	2 cups sugar
1 cup golden raisins	12 eggs, separated
1 cup coarsely chopped pecans	2 teaspoons vanilla extract
1 teaspoon cream of tartar	½ teaspoon mace
4 cups sifted flour	2 teaspoons grated lemon peel
1 pound (4 sticks) butter	Pinch of salt

1. Preheat the oven to 350 degrees. Grease two 9-inch tube pans and dust with flour.
2. Combine the candied fruit, raisins, and nuts in a bowl. Add the cream of tartar and 4 tablespoons of the flour. Toss lightly.
3. Cream the butter and ½ cup of the sugar until light and fluffy. Add the egg yolks, one at a time, beating well each time. Stir in the vanilla, mace, and grated lemon peel.
4. Add salt to the egg whites and beat in until they hold soft peaks. Add the remaining sugar, a tablespoon at a time, beating well after each addition, for a total of 5 minutes, or until the egg whites are very firm.
5. Thoroughly fold one quarter of the stiffly beaten egg whites into the creamed butter mixture. Pour the mixture back over the remaining egg whites. Sprinkle

the floured fruit on top. Fold all gently together, adding remaining flour at the same time.

6. Pour into prepared pans. Bake about 1 hour and 10 minutes, or until the cakes are golden brown and pull away from the sides of the pans.

YIELD: 24 SERVINGS

FRUITCAKE MAIL-ORDER CAPITAL OF THE WORLD: CORSICANA, TEXAS

The world's largest mail-order fruitcake operation is in the town of Corsicana, Texas (pop. 21,000). From here the Collins Street Bakery, which was founded in 1896, mails out four million pounds of fruitcake each year. It is owned by Bill McNutt, Jr., whose family took over the business in 1946 and who now runs it with his sons. Around the turn of the century, Corsicana was an oil boom town with a thriving opera house that brought in Enrico Caruso and Will Rogers and other stars of the day who stayed at the hotel above the bakery. In 1913, when the Ringling Brothers Circus was in town, circus executives staying at the hotel asked the manager to send some fruitcake to friends around the country as Christmas gifts, and the mail-order business began. Now, there are more than 400,000 mail-order customers for the cake, which is 28 percent Texan pecans, and includes pineapple from the bakery's plantations in Costa Rica, cherries from the Pacific Northwest, honey, eggs, butter, raisins from California, glacéed cherries, and no citron. Says Bill McNutt, Jr., "We don't know how to do it any better."

CAROLE WALTER'S
LIGHT FRUITCAKE

છ

This cake is made without leavening and is densely packed with a pretty combination of golden raisins, candied pineapple, glacéed red and green cherries, and nuts that look beautiful when the cake is sliced. It works well made in large batches that can be divided into mini-loaves for presents.

2 cups golden raisins
1 cup diced candied pineapple
¼ cup diced red glacéed cherries
¼ cup diced green glacéed cherries
2 tablespoons diced candied orange peel
2 tablespoons diced candied lemon peel
1 cup coarsely hand-chopped walnuts
½ cup coarsely hand-chopped blanched almonds
2¼ cups sifted unbleached all-purpose flour
½ teaspoon salt
½ pound (2 sticks) unsalted butter
½ teaspoon freshly grated navel orange peel

½ teaspoon freshly grated lemon peel
1 cup (lightly packed) light brown sugar
6 large eggs, separated
¼ cup maple syrup
¼ cup brandy, Grand Marnier, Cointreau, or Triple Sec, plus additional for brushing on finished cakes and for soaking cheesecloth
1½ teaspoons vanilla extract
1 teaspoon cream of tartar
Pinch of salt
2 tablespoons granulated sugar
2 tablespoons light corn syrup
2 teaspoons hot water
Almond halves and glacéed cherries for garnish (optional)

(continued)

1. Combine the fruits, candied peels, and nuts in a bowl.

2. Position rack in the lower third of the oven and preheat to 300 degrees. Butter two 8 x 4 x 2¼-inch loaf pans and line with brown paper.

3. Using a triple sifter, sift together the flour and salt. Remove ¼ cup and add to the fruits and nuts, tossing to coat the pieces well. Set the dry ingredients and the fruit mixture aside.

4. Cut the butter into 1-inch pieces and place in the large bowl of an electric mixer fitted with beaters or paddle attachment. Add the grated orange and lemon peels and soften on low speed. Increase speed to medium-high and cream until smooth and light in color, 1½ to 2 minutes.

5. Add the brown sugar, 1 tablespoon at a time, taking 3 to 4 minutes to blend it in well. Scrape the sides of the bowl occasionally.

6. Add the egg yolks, two at a time, at 1-minute intervals, scraping the sides of the bowl as necessary. Beat 1 minute longer.

7. Reduce mixer speed to low. In a small bowl, combine the maple syrup, brandy, and vanilla. Add a third of the flour mixture alternately with half the syrup mixture, beginning and ending with the flour. Mix for 10 seconds longer. Remove the bowl from the mixer and set aside.

8. In another large bowl of an electric mixer fitted with clean beaters or whip attachment, beat the egg whites on medium-high speed until frothy. Add the cream of tartar and salt. Increase the speed and beat until soft peaks form. Add the granulated sugar, 1 tablespoon at a time, and beat until mixture stands in firm peaks, 15 to 20 seconds.

9. Remove the bowl from the machine. Fold a third of the egg whites and half the fruit mixture into the batter, taking about 20 turns. Fold in remaining whites and fruit mixture, taking an additional 40 turns to combine.

10. Spoon the batter into prepared pans, smoothing the surface with the back of a

tablespoon. Tap the pans firmly to remove air pockets. Bake in the preheated oven for 1½ hours.

11. Five minutes before the end of the baking time, brush the top of each cake with the corn syrup thinned with hot water. If you wish, gently press halved almonds and glacéed cherries onto surface of cakes as a garnish.

12. Cakes are done when they begin to come away from the sides of the pans and a twig of straw or a toothpick inserted into the center comes out clean. Remove from oven, set the pans on cake racks, and let stand for half an hour. Turn the cakes onto their sides and ease them out of the pans. Carefully peel off paper and turn cakes top side up to finish cooling.

13. When cakes are completely cool, brush tops and sides with additional brandy. Wrap cakes in large pieces of brandy-soaked cheesecloth. You'll need ¼ to ⅓ cup brandy for each cake, depending on the size of the piece of cheesecloth. Double-wrap in heavy aluminum foil, sealing well. Allow cakes to mature for at least 6 weeks before serving.

YIELD: 12 TO 14 SERVINGS PER LOAF

Note:

Store the wrapped cakes in a cool dry place (a basement is ideal). Remoisten with rum after 2 days and again after 2 weeks. Check again for moistness after 1 month, but remoistening will probably no longer be necessary if cakes were well wrapped. They will keep for up to 6 months.

CANDIED LEMON, ORANGE, OR GRAPEFRUIT PEEL

❧

Candied peel should be cooked very slowly. This is based on a recipe by Nick Malgieri.

3 oranges, 4 lemons, or 1 large
   grapefruit
Sugar equal to the weight of the
   peel (2 cups per 1 pound peel)
Light corn syrup equal to half the
   weight of the sugar (1 cup per
   1 pound peel)

Water or lemon, orange, or
   grapefruit juice from the fruits
   equal to one fourth the weight
   of the sugar (½ cup per 1
   pound peel)

1. Score the fruit in 5 or 6 places from stem to blossom ends and remove the peel (both the colored part and the white part beneath it). Weight the pieces of peel. There should be about 1 pound.
2. Place the peel in a large saucepan or casserole and cover with water. Bring to a boil and drain. Repeat the process 7 more times to remove the bitterness from the peel and to soften it.
3. Combine the sugar, corn syrup, and water or juice in a large saucepan or casserole. Bring the syrup to a boil and add the blanched peel. Bring to a boil, lower to a simmer, and cook until the syrup is very thick. And ¼ cup water and return to a boil. Remove from heat and let cool.
4. Pack the candied peel, with its thick syrup, in plastic containers, cover tightly, and store in the refrigerator. Before using the peel, rinse under warm running water.

YIELD: ABOUT ¾ POUND

JANICE PIKE'S
WHITE FRUITCAKE

ℰℐ

The pineapple chunks in this fruitcake keep it moist. Marion Cunningham says it is an exceptionally good fruitcake—lighter, less rich, and easier to make than dark fruitcake. The cake is lovely all by itself and does not need to be doused with spirits.

2½ cups cake flour
1 teaspoon baking powder
½ teaspoon salt
1 cup candied cherries
2½ cups golden raisins
1 cup canned pineapple chunks, drained
1 cup coarsely chopped blanched almonds

1 cup coarsely chopped walnuts
½ pound (2 sticks) unsalted butter
1 cup sugar
5 eggs
1 teaspoon almond extract
2 teaspoons vanilla extract
2 teaspoons grated orange peel
2 teaspoons grated lemon peel

1. Preheat the oven to 275 degrees. Grease two 8½ x 4½ x 2½-inch loaf pans, line the sides and bottoms with heavy brown paper, parchment paper, or foil, then butter the paper or foil.

2. Combine the flour, baking powder, and salt and sift them together into a large mixing bowl. Add the cherries, raisins, pineapple, almonds, and walnuts and toss several times to coat them with the flour.

3. In another large mixing bowl, cream the butter and sugar until smooth and blended. Alternately blend the combined dry mixture and the eggs (two at a time) into the butter mixture in three stages (for the last addition you will have

(continued)

only 1 egg). Beat vigorously after each addition. Add the almond extract, vanilla, and orange and lemon peels and stir until thoroughly blended.

4. Pour the batter into the prepared pans, filling them to the top. Bake for about 2 hours, or until a broom straw inserted in the center of the cakes comes out clean.

5. Remove the cakes from the oven and let them cool in their pans for 30 minutes. Turn out onto a rack, peel off the paper, and let cool completely.

6. Wrap the cakes well and store them in an airtight container for up to 2 weeks. These do not have the keeping qualitites of dark fruitcake; if you are making them more than 2 weeks before serving, wrap well and freeze.

YIELD: ABOUT 12 SERVINGS PER LOAF

BILL NEAL'S
JAPANESE FRUITCAKE

Japanese fruitcake is not Japanese at all, but is a typically Southern dessert cake that was especially popular at the turn of the century. This same cake was once called Oriental cake, but there is nothing of the Far East about it except the spices—none of them Japanese in origin.

THE CAKE LAYERS

½ pound (2 sticks) unsalted
   butter, at room temperature
1⅞ cups sugar
4 eggs, separated, at room
   temperature
2⅔ cups all-purpose flour
2 teaspoons baking powder
⅔ teaspoon salt

1 cup milk
2 teaspoons vanilla extract
¼ cup brandy
1 teaspoon ground cinnamon
½ teaspoon ground cloves
1 teaspoon ground allspice
½ cup chopped raisins
½ cup chopped pecans

THE COCONUT FILLING

1 medium coconut
1½ cups sugar
2 tablespoons cornstarch
Pinch of salt

Grated zest and juice of 2 lemons
Whipped cream or Fluffy Icing
   (page 91)

(continued)

1. Preheat the oven to 350 degrees. Grease and flour four 9-inch cake pans.
2. Beat the butter until light and slowly add the sugar. Beat in the egg yolks one at a time, beating very well after each addition. This is the key to success: beat butter, sugar, and egg yolks very well until the mixture is very fluffy.
3. Sift together the flour, baking powder, and salt. Add one third to the butter mixture alternately with ½ cup milk, beginning and ending with the flour.
4. Beat the egg whites until stiff and fold into the batter. Stir in the vanilla and the brandy.
5. Divide the batter into two batches. Fill two of the pans with one batch. To the other batch add the spices, raisins, and nuts. Pour into the other two pans and bake all for 30 minutes in the preheated oven, until the tops are just golden brown and the edges pull slightly from the sides of the pan. Cool on a rack and turn out.
6. For the filling, drain the juice from the coconut and reserve. Crack the coconut, discard the outer shell, and pare away the brown skin. Grate the meat and put in a saucepan with the sugar. Measure the liquid from the coconut. If necessary, add water to make ¾ cup liquid and stir into the saucepan. Bring to a boil and cook about 5 minutes.
7. Dissolve the cornstarch in 2 tablespoons of coconut liquid if you have it, or water. Slowly add some of the hot liquid to the cornstarch, stir about, and stir back into the pot. Continue to cook at the simmer 3 or 4 more minutes. Season with a few grains of salt and lemon zest and juice. Set aside to cool, stirring occasionally.
8. To assemble, start with a dark layer. Spread with one third of the coconut filling. Alternate light with dark. Ice the outside of the cake with whipped cream or Fluffy Icing. The finished cake is sometimes sprinkled with more coconut.

YIELD: 16 SERVINGS

FLUFFY ICING

Fluffy icing is classically known as Italian meringue. It is easy to execute as long as one understands that the syrup must be hot enough to cook the egg whites as it is added. It can be flavored in a variety of ways according to one's taste or the nature of the cake. Raisins, currants, nuts, and coconut can be stirred in at the last minute.

1 cup sugar
⅓ cup water
¼ teaspoon cream of tartar
Pinch of salt
2 egg whites

1 teaspoon lemon juice, 1
teaspoon vanilla extract, or ½
teaspoon almond extract,
brandy, rum, or bourbon
½ cup chopped raisins, currants,
or pecans (optional)

1. Combine the sugar, water, cream of tartar, and salt in a saucepan; bring to a boil and cook 5 minutes.
2. Beat egg whites until frothy. Continue to beat and slowly pour the very hot syrup over the whites. Continue beating at high speed to form stiff, glossy peaks. Add the lemon juice or other flavorings and fruit or nuts if desired.

YIELD: ENOUGH TO FROST TOP AND SIDES OF THREE 9-INCH LAYERS (THE FOURTH DOES NOT GET FROSTED)

KEN HAEDRICH'S
RICOTTA FRUITCAKE

❧

Ricotta cheese and whole wheat flour are used for this unusual fruitcake, along with dried coconut and dark rum. It is a very elegant cake, and not too sweet.

"This is one of my favorite gift cakes. I've intentionally chosen light-colored fruits to keep the color scheme golden, but you can add dark fruit if you prefer. These fruits, however, do seem to have a particular affinity for the cake. As moist as this is, I've kept one in the fridge, wrapped in plastic wrap and overwrapped in foil, for more than a week and it was still in prime condition at that. The pans I specify are one of the common sizes available in supermarkets in disposable aluminum, but don't dispose of them when you're done."

1 cup chopped candied pineapple
1 cup golden raisins
1 cup coarsely chopped pecans
⅓ cup dark rum
½ pound (2 sticks) unsalted
*   butter, softened*
2 cups packed light brown sugar
6 large eggs, at room temperature
2 teaspoons vanilla extract
Finely grated peel of 2 lemons
2 cups unbleached flour

2 cups whole wheat pastry flour
1 tablespoon baking powder
1 teaspoon salt
1 teaspoon ground ginger
1 cup ricotta cheese
1¾ cups milk or light cream
⅔ cup unsweetened shredded
*   coconut (available at health*
*   food stores) or sweetened*
*   flaked coconut*
2 tablespoons unbleached flour

1. At least an hour before baking, preferably longer, combine the candied pineapple, raisins, pecans, and rum in a mixing bowl. Stir, then cover, periodically stirring to saturate the mixture thoroughly.

2. In the meantime, butter four 3¾ x 7¾-inch loaf pans and line them with buttered wax paper, buttered side out, letting the paper come over the edge by about 1 inch so that you can pull the cakes out easily later. Preheat the oven to 350 degrees.

3. In a large mixing bowl, cream the butter with an electric mixer, gradually beating in the brown sugar. Add the eggs, one at a time, beating well after each one. Beat in the vanilla and the lemon peel.

4. Sift the flours, baking powder, salt, and ginger into another bowl, adding any pieces of bran that remain in the sifter; set aside. Purée the ricotta cheese and the milk or cream in a blender.

5. Sift the dry ingredients into the creamed mixture, alternating with the ricotta mixture; do this in several stages, beginning and ending with the dry ingredients. Do not beat the batter.

6. Mix the coconut with the dried fruit and rum, then mix in the 2 tablespoons of flour. Fold the fruit mixture into the batter, then divide the batter evenly among the pans. Bake for 50 to 60 minutes, until a tester inserted in the center comes out clean. Cool the pans on a rack for 10 minutes, then lift them out by the wax paper. Cool for another 30 minutes, then carefully peel off the wax paper. As soon as the cakes no longer feel warm, wrap them in plastic wrap and overwrap in foil. Store in a cool location in an airtight container.

YIELD: ABOUT 32 SERVINGS

MOLASSES GINGER
FRUITCAKE

એ

Two cakes English people are very fond of are gingerbread and fruitcake. This recipe combines both in a cake that is light but that has an interesting fruit texture. It can be eaten immediately or kept for several months in a sealed tin.

3 cups all-purpose flour
2 teaspoons baking soda
1½ teaspoons ground ginger
¼ teaspoon salt
½ cup finely chopped crystallized
  ginger
⅓ cup chopped citron
⅓ cup chopped candied orange
  peel
½ cup dried cherries

½ cup currants
Fine dry bread crumbs or graham
  cracker crumbs for dusting pan
12 tablespoons (1½ sticks)
  unsalted butter
1 cup dark unsulfured molasses
¼ cup light brown sugar
¼ cup milk
3 large eggs

1. Sift the flour, baking soda, ginger, and salt into a large mixing bowl. Add the crystallized ginger, citron, candied orange peel, cherries, and currants. Toss well so that the fruit is lightly coated with the flour.

2. Preheat the oven to 325 degrees. Butter a 9¼ x 5¼ x 2½-inch loaf pan and sprinkle with bread crumbs. Shake out excess.

3. Combine the butter, molasses, and brown sugar in a small saucepan and cook over low heat until the butter has melted. Allow it to cool for 10 minutes, then add the milk. Stir, and beat in the eggs one by one.

4. Pour the molasses mixture into the bowl with the flour and fruit. Stir until the batter is mixed. Pour the batter into the prepared pan and bake the cake for 1 to 1¼ hours, or until it shrinks from the sides of the pan. A cake tester inserted in the center should come out clean.

5. Allow the cake to cool for 10 minutes in the pan. Invert the cake onto a rack and allow it to cool completely before serving.

YIELD: ABOUT 12 SERVINGS

Since making fruitcakes is a long, involved process, this is a nice time to recruit the children or other family members to help. It will put everyone in a festive holiday mood. On the day before you plan to bake the cake, the pans can be lined, the dry ingredients combined, and the fruit and nut preparations done. The easiest way to cut the fruit is by snipping the pieces with a pair of scissors. Don't try to chop it or the pieces will stick together. Chop the nuts coarsely by hand so they will be visible when you slice the cake.

To keep them from drying out during the long baking time, fruitcakes should be baked in moist heat. Place a large pan of water on the bottom shelf of the oven. An open roasting pan measuring about 10 x 14 x 2 inches is ideal; however, any pan will do as long as it is shallow enough to fit on the rack directly below the cake.

Carole Walter

CRAIG CLAIBORNE'S
WALNUT AND GINGER FRUITCAKE

❧

"I took my mother's favorite fruitcake and weighed separately the fruits and nuts used in her version. I substituted weight for weight candied ginger for her fruits and all walnuts for her mixed nuts. I think it is a great recipe."

½ pound candied ginger, cut into
⅛-inch cubes (about 1 cup)
1½ cups golden raisins
3¾ cups walnuts, preferably black
walnuts, broken into pieces
3 cups sifted all-purpose flour
1 teaspoon baking powder

Salt to taste
1 pound (4 sticks) butter, cut into
1-inch cubes
2 cups sugar
6 eggs, separated
⅓ cup Madeira or sweet sherry

1. Preheat the oven to 275 degrees. Lightly butter a 10-inch, 12-cup Bundt pan. Sprinkle with flour and shake pan to coat inside. Shake out excess.
2. In a mixing bowl, combine the ginger, raisins, and walnuts.
3. Sift together the flour, baking powder, and salt. Sift this mixture over ginger and nut mixture.
4. Put the butter in the bowl of an electric mixer. Start beating while gradually adding the sugar. Cream mixture well and gradually beat in egg yolks. Beat in Madeira.
5. Pour and scrape this mixture over nuts and blend the ingredients thoroughly. This is best done by hand.
6. Beat the egg whites until stiff and thoroughly fold in, until they do not show.

7. Pour the batter into the prepared pan and smooth over the top with a spatula. Set pan on a baking sheet and place in oven. Bake about 2¼ hours, or until cake is puffed above pan and nicely browned on top, or until internal temperature is 200 degrees on a thermometer.

8. Remove cake from pan shortly after baking. Tapping the bottom of the pan with a heavy knife will help. Store cake for at least 10 days. If desired, add an occasional touch more of Madeira or sherry (or Cognac or rum if desired). Keep closely covered, wrapped in cheesecloth or foil, and refrigerated until ready to use.

YIELD: 12 SERVINGS

CAMILLE GLEN'S JEWEL BOX CAKE

❧

This Southern cake is rich-tasting but not heavy, and it can be served year-round.

"If I had to choose only one fruitcake in all the world, it would be this one. It is as delicious as it is beautiful—what more could one ask? And it is lighter than most holiday cakes. For teas or receptions, it is lovely served with or without the frosting."

1 cup golden raisins
1¼ cups finely slivered glazed or
   dried apricots
½ cup finely chopped candied
   orange peel
½ cup finely chopped candied
   lemon peel
1 cup diced candied pineapple
   (4 rings)
½ cup plus 1½ tablespoons brandy
   or aged bourbon whiskey, plus
   more as needed
2⅔ cups sifted all-purpose flour
¼ teaspoon salt

2 teaspoons baking powder
½ pound (2 sticks) unsalted
   butter, cut into pieces
1½ cups sugar
6 large eggs, separated
¼ cup heavy or whipping cream
½ cup shredded tart apple
   (1 small apple)
¼ cup ground blanched almonds
   (see Note)
¼ cup chopped blanched almonds
¼ cup blanched pistachios or
   chopped citron
1½ teaspoons vanilla extract

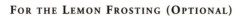

For the Lemon Frosting (Optional)

Peel of 1 lemon, finely chopped
2¾ cups confectioners' sugar,
*   sifted*
8 tablespoons (1 stick) butter, at
*   room temperature*

1 large egg yolk
Pinch of salt
2 tablespoons lemon juice, or
*   more to taste*

1. An hour or so before baking the cake, marinate the raisins, apricots, orange and lemon peels, and pineapple in the ½ cup brandy in a closed jar. Shake it several times.

2. Preheat the oven to 275 degrees. Grease a 10-inch tube pan and line it with foil.

3. Combine the sifted flour with the salt and baking powder and sift again.

4. Thoroughly cream the butter and 1 cup of the sugar with an electric mixer. Add the egg yolks and beat until the mixture is smooth.

5. Add the flour mixture in batches, alternating it with the cream. Beat it in by hand with a rubber spatula or with an electric mixer at very low speed.

6. Fold in the marinated fruit and brandy. If the fruit absorbed all of the brandy, add an additional 2 tablespoons or so of liquor to the cake batter. Fold in the apple, almonds, pistachios or citron, and vanilla.

7. Beat the egg whites until they hold soft peaks. Add the remaining ½ cup sugar and beat until they hold stiff peaks but are not dry and grainy. Fold a few spoonfuls into the batter by hand with a rubber spatula, then fold in the rest. If the batter looks the least bit curdled, fold in 2 or 3 extra tablespoons of sifted flour.

8. Spoon the batter into the pan, which should be no more than three-quarters full. Bake until the cake springs back at once when lightly touched, 2 to 2½ hours. A skewer or cake tester inserted into the center of the cake should come

(continued)

out clean. Remove the cake from the oven and brush the top with the 1½ tablespoons brandy or bourbon.

9. Run a thin sharp knife around the edge of the pan to loosen the cake, then unmold it onto a rack to cool.

10. Serve the cake as is or, when cool, frost the top and sides with lemon frosting in a swirling design. To make the frosting, combine the lemon peel, confectioners' sugar, and butter. Cream together with the egg, salt, and lemon juice. If frosting is too stiff, add an additional teaspoon of lemon juice.

YIELD: 12 TO 16 SERVINGS

Note:

Almonds should be ground in a Mouli or other rotary grater, not in a food processor. Done in a processor, nuts are likely to become oily. The almonds for this recipe should be very dry.

FAVORITE
EUROPEAN
FRUITCAKES

Fruitcakes have been popular in Europe since Roman times, when a version was made that consisted of raisins, pine nuts, and pomegranate seeds mixed into barley mash. In the Middle Ages, sweet ingredients such as honey, dried fruits, and spices were added to bread dough for special occasions, since dried fruit was an expensive luxury. In England in the seventeenth century, fruitcakes were called plum cakes (not to be confused, as they often are in the United States, with plum pudding, the steamed pudding served with hard sauce)—although they never contained any plums. Until the end of the eighteenth century, there were even laws on the books restricting the making of this kind of bread to celebrations such as Christmas, Easter, weddings, christenings, and funerals.

In England, fruitcakes for Christmas are started in the fall, at the same time as the Christmas puddings. Like the puddings, the cakes are better aged and should, if possible, be made at least a couple of months before Christmas. Then they are wrapped in cheesecloth soaked in brandy and kept in a cool dark place until the holidays. It is virtually impossible to age a fruitcake for too long—some people make theirs a year in advance. If they are stored in airtight containers and basted from time to time with liquor, they keep indefinitely. Toasted almonds, marzipan, or sprigs of holly go on top of the cakes, which at Christmastime are almost black, piled with marzipan and spread with a hard frosting that is made to look like snow, on which a Santa Claus with reindeer and sleigh is placed. In Great Britain, a similar dark, aged fruitcake is served at weddings. One year, when I was twelve, I received in the mail a chunk of black fruitcake topped with marzipan and white icing dotted with tiny edible silver balls the size of pearls. It was from the bride whose wedding I had been unable to attend. The piece of fruitcake, according to tradition, was to be put under my pillow so that I would dream of the man I would marry.

In Ireland, a popular fruitcake is made with Guinness beer. Dried fruit is soaked overnight in the beer, and after the cake is cooked, more beer is poured into holes made in the bottom of the cake while it is still hot. The British make a similar cake using sherry.

In Italy, a popular Christmas dessert sold in specialty shops and bakeries is *panforte,* a thin fruitcake, rich as candy, that is dense, chewy, and slightly spicy. It comes from Siena, where it was first made about a thousand years ago. It is still made there today, but manufacturers keep their recipes a closely guarded secret.

In Germany, loaves of fruitbread decorated with almonds and cherries are sold around Christmastime. *Hutzelbrot* is a cakelike bread made with dried pears and other fruits. It is sometimes served for breakfast, or with tea or coffee. It is at its best when sliced thin and spread with butter—and it keeps for about two months.

A Fruitcake Theory

by Calvin Trillin

৵৲

December 19, 1988

This was the year I was going to be nice about fruitcake. "Just try to be nice," my wife said. My younger daughter—the one who is still in high school and talks funny—said the same thing. Actually, what she said was, "Cool it, Pops. Take a chill on the fruitcake issue." That's the same thing.

They were right. I knew they were right. It's not that I hadn't tried to be nice before. It's not my fault that some years ago I happened to pass along a theory about fruitcake I had heard from someone in Denver. The theory was that there is only one fruitcake, and that this fruitcake is simply sent on from year to year. It's just a theory.

But every year around this time, someone calls up and says something like, "I'm doing a story on people who make fun of the holiday symbols that so many Americans hold dear—symbols that do so much for warm family life in this great country of ours and remain so very meaningful to all decent people. You're the one who maligns fruitcake, right?"

"Well, it's just a theory," I always mutter. "Something someone in Denver said once."

Who in Denver? Well, I can't remember. I'm always hearing theories from people in Denver. People in Denver are stinky with theories.

I don't know why. It may be because of the altitude, although that's just a theory.

Anyway, I can't be expected to remember the name of every single person in Denver who ever laid a theory on me. I've had people in Denver tell me that if you play a certain Rolling Stones record backward you get detailed instructions on how to dismantle a 1977 Volkswagen Rabbit. A man I once met in a bar in Denver told me that the gases produced by the drying of all these sun-dried tomatoes were causing the earth to wobble on its axis in a way that will put every pool table in the western hemisphere nearly a bubble off level by the end of this century. Don't get me started on people in Denver and their theories.

The point is that nobody ever interviews the person who gave me the theory about fruitcake, because nobody wants to start picking through this gaggle of theory-mongers in Denver to find him. So I was the one called up this year by someone who said he was doing a piece about a number of Scrooge-like creatures who seemed to derive sadistic pleasure out of trashing some of our most treasured American holiday traditions.

"Well, come right over," I said. "It's always nice to be included."

He said he'd catch me the next afternoon, just after he finished interviewing a guy who never passes a Salvation Army Santa Claus without saying, "Hiya, lard-gut."

When he arrived, I remembered that I was going to try to take a chill on the fruitcake issue. I told him that the theory about there only being one fruitcake actually came from somebody in Denver, maybe the same guy who talked to me at length about his theory that dinosaurs became extinct because they couldn't adapt to the personal income tax.

Then, trying for a little historical perspective, I told him about a family in Michigan I once read about that brings out an antique fruitcake every Christmas, a fruitcake that for some reason was not eaten at Christmas dinner in 1895 and has symbolized the holidays ever since. They put it on the table, not as dessert but as something between an icon and a centerpiece. "It's a very sensible way to use a fruitcake," I said. I was trying to be nice.

"You mean you think that fruitcake would be dangerous to eat?" he asked.

"Well, you wouldn't eat an antique," I said. "My Uncle Ralph used to chew on an old sideboard now and then, but we always considered it odd behavior."

"Would a fruitcake that isn't an antique be dangerous?"

"You mean a reproduction?"

"I mean a modern fruitcake."

"There's nothing dangerous about fruitcakes as long as people send them along without eating them," I said, in the nicest sort of way. "If people ever started eating them I suppose there might be need for federal legislation."

"How about people who buy fruitcakes for themselves?" he asked.

"Well, now that you mention it," I said, "nobody in the history of the United States has ever bought a fruitcake for himself. People have bought turnips for themselves. People have bought any number of Brussels sprouts for themselves. But no one has ever bought a fruitcake for himself. That does tell you a little something about fruitcakes."

"Are you saying that everybody secretly hates fruitcake?" he asked.

"Well, it's just a theory."

from *Enough's Enough*

JANE GRIGSON'S
COUNTRY CHRISTMAS CAKE

჻

This is the dark, rich, deeply traditional English Christmas cake I remember eating as a child at Christmas and weddings in England. To be at its best, it should be aged for a few months. It is finished with marzipan and icing to create a snowy effect.

7 cups (2½ pounds) mixed dried fruit (raisins, pitted prunes, figs)

½ cup (2 ounces) candied peel

½ cup (2 ounces) candied cherries, rinsed and halved

¾ cup (3 ounces) chopped candied or preserved ginger

Grated peel and juice of 1 large orange

Grated peel and juice of 1 large lemon

1 tablespoon bitter orange marmalade

1 tablespoon apricot jam

1 cup applesauce

2 tablespoons sweet sherry

3 cups all-purpose flour

1 teaspoon ground cinnamon

1 teaspoon ground ginger

1 teaspoon baking powder

1 teaspoon grated nutmeg

1 teaspoon ground cloves

1 teaspoon ground allspice

½ pound (2 sticks) unsalted butter

1 cup dark brown sugar

4 eggs

1 teaspoon pure vanilla extract

Few drops of almond extract

2 to 3 tablespoons whiskey or brandy

(continued)

1. The day before making the cake, finely chop the raisins, prunes, figs, candied peel, candied cherries, and ginger. Add the peel and juice of the orange and lemon along with the marmalade and jam. Add the applesauce and sherry, mix thoroughly, cover, and allow to steep overnight.
2. Preheat the oven to 325 degrees. Line the bottom and side of a deep 8- or 9-inch springform pan with 3 layers of parchment.
3. Sift together the flour, cinnamon, ginger, baking powder, nutmeg, cloves, and allspice. Cream the butter with the sugar until fluffy. Beat in the eggs, one at a time, and the vanilla and almond extracts. Mix the fruit and flour alternately into the butter mixture.
4. Pour the batter into the pan and bake for 2 hours. Lower the temperature to 300 degrees and bake for another 2 hours. If your oven temperature is unstable, check it frequently.
5. Take the cake out of the oven, pierce it all over with a skewer, and pour over it the whiskey or brandy. Let it cool in the pan, then remove it, peel off the parchment, wrap the cake in wax paper, place it in an airtight tin, and leave it in a cool dry place for at least a month before serving.
6. When the time comes to decant the cake, glaze it and cover it with marzipan. Then ice the cake with Royal Icing (page 110), if you like.

MARZIPAN (ALMOND PASTE)

½ pound confectioners' sugar	*1 large egg*
1 pound ground almonds	*3 to 4 teaspoons lemon juice*

GLAZE

1 tablespoon apricot jam	*1 tablespoon water*

1. Sift the confectioners' sugar and mix it with the almonds.
2. Beat the egg thoroughly; add the lemon juice and the dry ingredients. Use a wooden spoon to beat everything to a firm paste, then knead it on a board or Formica surface that has been sprinkled with confectioners' sugar.
3. Slice the top from the cake to make it even, then turn it upside down and put it on a wire rack. Boil the jam and water in a small pan, sieve it into a bowl, and while still hot, brush it over the top of the cake (that is, over what *was* the bottom).
4. Set aside a third of the almond paste and roll out the rest to a circle just a little larger than the cake—do this on a sheet of clean greaseproof paper, using the cake tin as a guide. Press the glazed side of the cake down on to the circle of marzipan; reverse it so that you now have the greaseproof paper on top, then the marzipan and then the cake. Remove the paper and smooth the marzipan down over the sides.
5. Measure the depth of the cake and its circumference. Roll out the remaining marzipan to these measurements, again on a sheet of greaseproof paper. Brush the cake sides with apricot glaze and roll it slowly along the strip of marzipan. Pat everything into place, closing the cracks and so on, and replace the cake on its rack. Leave for 2 days before icing it.

YIELD: 20 SERVINGS

ROYAL ICING

2 small egg whites
2 teaspoons lemon juice

1 pound confectioners' sugar

1. Whisk the egg whites until they are white and foamy, but not stiff. Stir in the lemon juice, then the sugar, which should be sieved. Do this bit by bit, using a wooden spoon. When everything is mixed together, continue to beat the mixture until it is a dazzling white. Cover the bowl and leave it for an hour or two before using it.

2. To ice the cake, put a bowl of hot water beside it. Put about half the icing on the cake and spread it about with a palette knife, which you have dipped in the water. It should be hot and wet, but not wet enough to soak the cake and ruin the icing. Cover the cake all over, then put on the remaining icing, either roughly to make a snowy effect, or in an elegant design with the aid of a pastry bag and nozzles.

YIELD: ENOUGH TO ICE TOP AND SIDES OF ONE 9-INCH CAKE

Fruitcake, the richest of all English cakes, was called plum cake for centuries. . . . These cakes held pounds and pounds of cut peel and dried fruit . . . raisins, sultanas or golden raisins and particularly currants (for which this island has shown a violent fondness since Roman times), all supported in a yeast dough and baked in freehand shapes or metal hoops in the old bread ovens.

Helen Simpson, *The London Ritz Book of Afternoon Tea*

NICK MALGIERI'S
OXFORD FRUITCAKE

၈၅

This is a particularly sumptuous dark fruitcake. Full of rum and dark, potent spices, it is brightened with a wrapping of marzipan and served in bite-size squares. Malgieri adapted the recipe from a traditional English fruitcake baked by Daphne Giles, his friend from Newbury, near Oxford.

2 cups (½ pound) each: dark raisins, golden raisins, currants, dates, dried figs, and mixed candied fruits

1 cup (¼ pound) each: candied cherries, candied pineapple, walnut halves, pecan halves, and whole almonds

1 cup dark rum plus ½ cup (optional) for aging the fruitcake

2¼ cups unbleached, all-purpose flour

1 teaspoon each: baking powder, ground cinnamon, grated nutmeg, and salt

½ teaspoon each: baking soda and ground cloves

½ pound (2 sticks) unsalted butter

1 cup (firmly packed) dark brown sugar

4 large eggs

1 pound almond paste (available canned), cut into half-inch pieces

1 pound confectioners' sugar, plus more for rolling out the marzipan

1 cup light corn syrup

1. Pit the dates, stem the figs, and cut both into half-inch pieces. Cut the pineapple into half-inch pieces, mix it with the other candied fruits in a large strainer, and rinse under cold water. Combine all the fruits and nuts in a bowl with a capacity of at least 6 quarts and sprinkle with ½ cup of the rum. Leave tightly covered for several days or proceed immediately to the next step.

2. Preheat the oven to 300 degrees. Butter a 12 x 18-inch baking pan (at least an inch high) and line it with parchment paper.

3. Sift the flour with the spices, salt, baking powder, and baking soda.

4. In a mixer, beat the butter until light, add the brown sugar, and beat until fluffy. Beat in 2 of the eggs, then half the flour mixture, then the other 2 eggs, and finally the rest of the flour mixture. Pour and scrape this thick batter over the fruit and nuts and fold them together thoroughly. Press the batter evenly into the prepared baking pan. Place another piece of parchment paper over the batter and press well to adhere.

5. Bake for 1 hour; the top of the fruitcake under the parchment paper will lose its shiny, sticky quality and will resist the pressure of your fingertips. Cool in the pan, remove the parchment paper cover, and cut it crosswise into two fruitcakes to make it easier to handle. Unmold the fruitcakes, sprinkling both the top and the bottom with ½ cup of the rum. Proceed immediately to the following paragraph, or if you wish to age the fruitcake, moisten two pieces of rinsed cheesecloth with an additional ½ cup of rum, wrap them around the cakes, wrap the cakes in plastic and then in foil, and leave them for several days, weeks, or longer.

6. When ready to serve, combine the almond paste, confectioners' sugar, and ½ cup of the corn syrup in a food processor fitted with the metal blade and pulse 10 or 12 times; the result will be a coarse, mealy marzipan. Gather and knead the

marzipan by hand until it is smooth, divide it into four equal balls, and wrap them tightly in plastic wrap.

7. Bring the other ½ cup corn syrup to a boil and brush about a quarter of it on top of the fruitcake. On a surface dusted with confectioners' sugar, roll one ball of marzipan to the size of the fruitcake, lift the marzipan sheet off the surface, and press it well onto the top of the fruitcake. Repeat with the other fruitcake.

8. Turn both fruitcakes over onto a clean surface, brush them with the remaining corn syrup, roll out the two remaining balls of marzipan, and press them onto the fruitcakes. Trim the edges and cut the fruitcakes into 2-inch squares.

YIELD: 54 SMALL SERVINGS

ↄↄ

The lion and the unicorn
Were fighting for the crown;
The lion beat the unicorn
All around the town.
Some gave them white bread
And some gave them brown;
And some gave them plum cake,
And sent them out of town.
Old nursery rhyme

ↄↄ

BRIGADIER ANNE FIELD'S KESWICK FRUITCAKE

e/s

This recipe comes from my father's side of the family, who are from Keswick in the Lake District. It was given to me by my cousin, who recently retired as head of the W.R.A.C. When I visit my parents, who now live in London, she often brings us her delicious fruitcake.

2 cups white raisins
1 cup candied peel
2 cups mixed chopped glacéed
    pineapple, papaya, or other
    glacéed fruit except cherries
1 cup chopped walnuts
¼ cup ground almonds
¾ cup glacéed cherries, rinsed and
    chopped

½ cup Cognac or rum
½ pound (2 sticks) unsalted butter
2 cups sugar
4 eggs
2 cups all-purpose flour
1 teaspoon baking powder
½ teaspoon salt
1 lemon
Grated peel of 1 orange

1. A day in advance of making the cake, put the white raisins, peel, and glacéed fruits (except the cherries) in a bowl. Add the walnuts and ground almonds and mix well into the fruit. Place the cherries in a bowl with the Cognac.
2. On the day of making the cake, preheat the oven to 325 degrees.
3. Cream the butter with the sugar until light colored. Add the eggs one at a time and blend in thoroughly. Sift in the flour, baking powder, and salt. Grate the peel from the lemon and squeeze the juice from it.
4. Fold in the fruit and nuts, the lemon peel and orange peel, and mix thoroughly.

Add the cherries soaked in Cognac and the lemon juice. Mix well.

5. Line one 8-inch round or square tin with wax paper, greasing the tin and paper. Spoon the mixture into the tin so that the top is flat (you can do this by knocking the tin gently on the working surface). Place the tin in the low center of the oven.

6. Bake for 1 hour, turn down heat to 300 degrees, and bake for another 1½ hours, or until cooked. Test by piercing the center of the cake with a skewer. It should come out clean when the cake is ready. When the cake is cool, wrap in the lining and aluminum foil and store in a tin and a sealed plastic container. The cake will keep in a cool place for a couple of months.

YIELD: ABOUT 20 SERVINGS

In England it is still the custom for unmarried guests at a wedding to put a piece of the cake (traditionally a dark fruitcake) under their pillow at night. It's said they will dream of the person they are to marry.

JANE GARMEY'S DUNDEE CAKE

❧

Since my family is from near Dundee, we often had this cake when I was growing up. It was as much a part of afternoon tea as brown bread and butter and chocolate biscuits.

"The city was and still is famous not just for its marmalade, but also for its plum cake, which is rich and fruity and covered with almonds," says Jane Garmey. One of its virtues is that it keeps well (for a couple of months), stored in an airtight container.

½ cup white raisins
½ cup dark raisins
½ cup currants
¼ cup candied fruit peel
6 candied cherries, finely chopped
½ cup ground almonds
½ pound (2 sticks) butter
1 cup sugar

Grated peel of 1 orange
4 eggs
2¼ cups all-purpose flour
1 teaspoon baking powder
1 tablespoon sherry
¼ cup blanched almonds, split
    lengthwise into halves

1. Preheat the oven to 300 degrees. Grease an 8-inch cake pan at least 3 inches high and line it with greased wax paper.
2. Mix together the raisins, currants, peel, cherries, and ground almonds in a bowl and set aside.
3. Cream the butter and sugar and add the orange peel. Beat the eggs separately and gradually add them to the mixture, beating well. Sift the flour and baking

powder and fold them into the mixture. Add the sherry and all the fruit. Pour into the cake pan and arrange the almonds on top in circles.

4. Bake for 2 to 2½ hours, or until a knife comes out clean.

5. Allow the cake to cool for 10 minutes and then turn it onto a wire rack and cool fully before serving.

YIELD: 10 TO 12 SERVINGS

COTSWOLDS SHERRY
FRUITCAKE

ᧇ

A popular English fruitcake, particularly in the Cotswolds, where it is traditionally eaten after a day at the hunt. The day after Christmas in England is a holiday known as Boxing Day, and in many country villages it is a major occasion, when hounds and huntsmen meet for the hunt.

8 tablespoons (1 stick) unsalted
   butter
1 cup sugar
3 eggs
2 cups flour
½ teaspoon baking powder
½ teaspoon salt
1 cup ground almonds

¼ pound candied peel
½ cup glacéed cherries
1 cup currants, soaked overnight
   in 1 cup dry sherry
2 tablespoons whole almonds,
   blanched
¾ cup dry sherry

1. Preheat the oven to 325 degrees. Grease an 8-inch round cake tin and line it with wax paper.
2. Cream the butter with the sugar in a mixing bowl until light and fluffy.
3. Separate the eggs and beat in the yolks.
4. Sift the flour and the baking powder and gradually fold them into the butter-sugar mixture with the salt. Mix well and add the ground almonds, candied peel, and cherries. Add the currants with their soaking sherry.
5. Beat the egg whites until stiff and fold them into the batter.
6. Pour the batter into the prepared pan and decorate the top with whole almonds.

(continued)

Bake for 1 hour, then turn the heat down to 300 degrees. Bake for 1 hour longer.

7. While the cake is still hot, pour the ¾ cup sherry over by spoonfuls and leave until the cake is cool. Cover with sherry-soaked cheesecloth.

YIELD: 10 TO 12 SERVINGS

GUINNESS FRUITCAKE

ᐰ

In Ireland, a popular fruitcake is made using Guinness beer. Dried fruit is soaked overnight in the beer, and after the cake is baked, more beer is poured into holes made in the bottom of the hot cake.

8 tablespoons (1 stick) unsalted
    butter
1 cup dark brown sugar
3 eggs, lightly beaten
2¼ cups flour
1 teaspoon baking powder
1 teaspoon ground allspice

½ teaspoon salt
1 cup raisins, soaked overnight in
    1 cup Guinness beer
½ cup candied peel
½ cup chopped walnuts
1 cup Guinness beer

1. Preheat the oven to 325 degrees. Grease an 8-inch round cake tin and line with buttered wax paper.
2. Cream the butter and sugar in a mixing bowl until light and fluffy. Beat in the eggs.
3. Sift the flour and baking powder and gradually fold with the allspice into the butter-sugar mixture. Add the salt, drained raisins, candied peel, and walnuts. Mix thoroughly.
4. Bake for 1 hour at 325 degrees. Turn down heat to 300 degrees and bake for an additional 1 to 1¼ hours.
5. Remove the cake from the oven and let it cool. Remove it from the cake pan and turn it upside down. Using a skewer, make holes around the bottom of the cake and pour in the cup of Guinness. To store, wrap in muslin or cheesecloth

soaked in Guinness and put in a sealed tin or tightly wrapped foil. Keep in a cool place.

YIELD: 10 TO 12 SERVINGS

SEBASTIAN THOMAS'S SODA CAKE

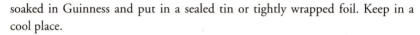

When Sebastian Thomas gave me this recipe I thought it looked familiar. In fact, it is light and spicy, just like a cake my Irish grandmother used to make for tea when I was growing up. We used to spread slices of it with butter. The recipe was given to Thomas by an Englishwoman who claimed it was handed down from generation to generation. It *is* as old as World War II, however, since the original instructions called for using more vinegar and milk in case there were no eggs available.

2⅔ cups all-purpose flour	*⅛ teaspoon ground ginger*
12 tablespoons (1½ sticks)	*⅛ teaspoon grated nutmeg*
unsalted butter, lard, or	*⅛ teaspoon ground cloves*
margarine	*⅛ teaspoon ground cinnamon*
2 cups currants or sultanas	*1½ cups milk*
1 firmly packed cup moist brown	*1 teaspoon baking soda*
sugar	*1 tablespoon malt vinegar*
½ cup candied peel	*1 egg (optional)*

1. Preheat the oven to 350 degrees.
2. Grease the bottom of an 8-inch cake pan and line it with wax paper.
3. Rub butter into the flour with the tips of your fingers until it resembles bread crumbs. Add the currants or sultanas, sugar, candied peel, and spices.
4. Warm 1 cup of the milk and add the baking soda. Stir until amalgamated, then add the remaining milk, the vinegar, and the optional egg. Pour quickly onto the dry ingredients. Mix thoroughly.
5. Pour into prepared pan and bake for 1½ to 2 hours, or until a skewer inserted in the center comes out clean. Cool on a rack. The cake keeps for about a week.

YIELD: 10 TO 12 SERVINGS

HORST SCHARFENBERG'S PEAR FRUITCAKE

⌘

This rich German fruit bread—also known as *Hutzelbrot, Schnitzbrot, Bierewecke* ("pear rolls"), or just plain *Fruchtebrot* (fruit bread)—contains nuts, orange and lemon peels, and raisins. *Hutzeln* (pear pieces dried with the skin still on) show up in the grocery stores in Baden every fall, but people often choose their pears and supervise the drying process themselves. The quantities involved in this recipe are quite substantial, since the family supply of *Hutzelbrot* was supposed to last from late fall until Groundhog Day (better known in Germany as *Lichtmess,* or Candlemas), February 2.

3¼ pounds dried pears (include
    some dried figs and pitted
    prunes if you like)
4 cups flour
2 tablespoons lukewarm milk
3¼ teaspoons yeast
1 cup plus 2 tablespoons sugar
Pinch of salt
1¼ cups sultana raisins, rinsed
    and dried
4 cups whole hazelnuts or
    walnuts, coarsely chopped

⅓ cup diced candied orange peel
⅓ cup diced candied lemon peel
½ teaspoon ground cinnamon
½ teaspoon ground cloves
1 tablespoon fennel seed or
    aniseed
3 to 4 tablespoons kirsch (cherry
    liqueur)
1 tablespoon cornstarch

1. Remove the stems from the pears, rinse the pears and other dried fruit, soak in enough water to cover for a couple of hours, then coarsely chop the dried fruit and cook in the soaking liquid for about 30 minutes. Keep the cover on the pot and let stand overnight.

2. The next day, start by sifting the flour into a large mixing bowl. Make a crater in the flour. Place 2 tablespoons lukewarm milk in it and sprinkle the yeast over the milk. Dust the yeast with flour and let it stand for 15 minutes. Then add the 1 cup sugar, the salt, dried fruit, and 1 cup of the cooking liquid (reserving the remainder). Knead into a dough. Work the raisins and nut meats into the dough, along with the candied orange and lemon peels, the spices, and the kirsch. Do not knead too vigorously, however, or the dough is likely to get overworked and pulpy.

3. Transfer the dough mass to a second mixing bowl, the inside of which has been coated with a thick layer of flour, and roll the dough back and forth until it no longer sticks to the sides; sprinkle with a little more flour from time to time, if necessary. Cover the bowl with a damp towel and let the dough stand until cracks or "stretch marks" start to appear in the surface (40 minutes to 2 hours).

4. Preheat the oven to 400 degrees. Grease a baking sheet. Separate the dough mass into 6–8 small loaves. Place these on the baking sheet, then let stand for 1 hour before baking.

5. Measure about 2 cups of the reserved liquid in which the dried fruit was soaked and cooked, add the remaining 2 tablespoons sugar, and bring to a boil, then stir in the cornstarch. Brush the loaves of *Hutzelbrot* with this mixture while they are still warm. If you like, the loaves can also be garnished with almond halves, which will stick on very nicely if pressed into the warm glaze. Adding a little extra kirsch to the glaze gives the *Hutzelbrot* a nice Black Forest flavor.

(continued)

Cultural Note: *Das Stuttgarter Hutzelmännlein* ("The Little Pear Man of Stuttgart") is a famous folk tale by Eduard Mörike about a shoemaker's apprentice who is rewarded with a *Hutzelbrot* that during the night grows again to its original size—no matter how much one has eaten. The *Hutzelbrot* you'll bake will probably be eaten in a very short time—but, sorry, it won't grow during the night!

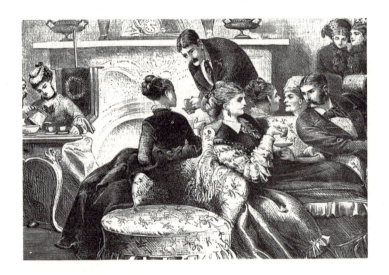

It is well worth making the candied orange peel from scratch for this version of *panforte*. The cake is rich and chewy, and the quality of the fruit in it makes all the difference.

"Siena's many pastry shops prepare an array of different *panforti,* chewy distant cousins of fruitcake," says Malgieri. Although recipes abound, none of Siena's *panforte* manufacturers will reveal the recipe. This version comes from my memory of eating much *panforte* in Siena and from Giovanni Righi Parenti's wonderful chapter on *panforte* in *La Grande Cucina Toscana.*

"Old recipes for *panforte* do not contain honey as an ingredient, because formerly a special type of candied fruit, fermented in a honey syrup, was used in the dough. Nowadays honey is added to the dough to produce a similar flavor.

"Usually the *panforte* is baked in a mold lined with edible wafer paper, called *ostia* in Italian and *oblaten* in German. Stores that carry German and Eastern European foods carry *oblaten* for making traditional Christmas cakes and cookies. It can be obtained from Paprika Weiss, 1546 Second Avenue, New York, NY 10028 (212) 288-6117. You can also use Chinese edible rice paper, available in Asian markets, which will produce equally good results."

See the recipe for candied orange peel (page 86) if you want to start from scratch.

(continued)

Edible wafer paper
⅔ cup honey
⅔ cup sugar
¾ cup diced candied citron or melon
¾ cup diced candied orange peel
1½ cups whole blanched almonds, lightly toasted

¾ cup plus 2 tablespoons all-purpose flour
1 plus ½ teaspoon ground cinnamon
¼ teaspoon ground coriander
¼ teaspoon ground cloves
¼ teaspoon grated nutmeg
Confectioners' sugar

1. Butter a 10-inch tart pan with a removable bottom. Line the bottom of the pan with edible paper or parchment. If using parchment, butter it. Preheat the oven to 300 degrees.

2. Combine the honey and sugar in a saucepan and stir to mix. Place over low heat and bring to a boil. Simmer the mixture for 2 minutes after it comes to a boil, without stirring.

3. While the sugar and honey are heating, combine the candied fruit and almonds in a heatproof mixing bowl. In another bowl, combine the ¾ cup flour with spices (reserving ½ teaspoon cinnamon) and stir to mix. Pour the honey-and-sugar syrup over the fruit mixture, add the flour mixture, and stir vigorously to combine. Immediately scrape the dough out of the bowl into the prepared pan. Wet the palm of one hand and press the dough into place. Do not press too hard, since the dough will still be fairly hot. Make the top of the *panforte* as flat as possible. Combine the 2 tablespoons flour and remaining cinnamon and sift over the top of the *panforte* through a small, fine strainer.

4. Bake for about 20 minutes, checking occasionally that the dough does not come to a boil. Cool on a rack for 10 minutes, then loosen the *panforte* from the side of the pan with the tip of a small knife and remove the side of the pan. Slide a

knife or spatula between the *panforte* and the pan bottom and slide the cake onto a rack to cool completely. If parchment was used, invert the *panforte* and peel off the paper after the cake has completely cooled; then reinvert.

5. Brush the flour and cinnamon away from the top of the *panforte* and dust it with the confectioners' sugar before serving.

6. Keep the *panforte* in a tightly covered tin at room temperature; it will stay fresh for a month.

YIELD: 8 TO 10 SERVINGS

MAIDA HEATTER'S
PANFORTE CIOCCOLATO

&

When I asked Maida Heatter for a recipe for this book, she responded by sending me this cake. It was one of the most delicious cakes I have ever eaten and I found myself creeping into the kitchen late at night for another nibble.

"I have many favorite fruitcakes, but this is my numero uno," she says. "*Panforte* was originally made in Siena, Italy, about one thousand years ago—and it is still made there. The religious crusaders carried it with them on their expeditions, not only because it is so good and so satisfying, but also because it lasts so very well. Nowadays you will see *panforte* in better food stores, especially at Christmastime (it does make a perfect gift), but make it anytime, it is always a special treat. Simple, but sophisticated and elegant. Chewy, crunchy, and like caramel candy. Not too sweet. Slightly spicy.

"Although the translation of *panforte* is 'strong bread,' this is a fruitcake. It is shallow (a scant 1 inch high), almost solid fruits and nuts, with barely enough batter (a chocolate honey batter) to hold it all together. It is wonderful."

*1 cup blanched or unblanched
    (natural) and toasted almonds*
Fine dry bread crumbs for pan
*½ cup (loosely packed) diced
    glazed orange peel*
*½ cup (loosely packed) diced
    glazed lemon peel*

*½ cup (loosely packed) diced
    glazed citron*
½ cup unsifted unbleached flour
*⅓ cup unsweetened cocoa powder
    (preferably Dutch process)*
1 teaspoon ground cinnamon
¼ teaspoon ground allspice

¼ teaspoon white pepper
1½ teaspoons powdered instant
  espresso or coffee
1 cup blanched and lightly
  toasted hazelnuts

½ cup mild honey
½ cup granulated sugar
Confectioners' sugar

1. To toast the almonds, preheat the oven to 350 degrees. Place the almonds in a shallow cake pan and bake in the center of the oven, stirring once or twice, for 12 to 15 minutes. Set aside.
2. Move a rack to the lower third of the oven and lower the temperature to 325 degrees. Cut a round of parchment to fit the bottom of a 9-inch springform pan, 2 or 3 inches deep. Cut a strip (or two shorter strips) about 1½ inches wide to go around the sides of the pan. Butter the sides and bottom of the pan. First place the strip (or strips) around the sides of the pan, just touching the bottom and covering only part of the way up on the sides. Then place the round in the bottom of the pan. Butter the papers on the bottom and the sides, dust all over with fine dry bread crumbs, invert over paper to shake out excess crumbs, and set the pan aside.
3. Place all the glazed fruits in a large mixing bowl. Sift together over the fruit the flour, cocoa, cinnamon, allspice, white pepper, and espresso or coffee powder. With your hands, mix the fruits with the dry ingredients, thoroughly separating and coating the pieces. Add the almonds and hazelnuts and mix again. Set aside.
4. Place the honey and sugar in a saucepan with a 6-cup capacity over moderate heat. Stir with a wooden spatula until the sugar is dissolved and the mixture comes to a boil. Then insert a candy thermometer in the pan and let the mixture boil without stirring until the thermometer registers 248 degrees (stiff-ball stage); the mixture will reach this temperature soon after it comes to a boil.

5. Now you must work very quickly before the hot syrup cools and hardens. Pour the syrup onto the fruit mixture, stir with a heavy wooden spatula to mix, and— without waiting—transfer the mixture to the prepared pan. (There will be just barely enough syrup to moisten the dry ingredients.)

6. Immediately cover with a piece of plastic wrap and press down on the top with your hands to press the mixture into an even layer. Then use a can or a small saucepan or any round and flat piece of equipment to press down very firmly on top to form a compact layer. Quickly remove the plastic wrap.

7. Bake for 40 minutes. (You will not know by looking or testing that the cake is done; it will become firm as it cools.) Do not overbake.

8. Set aside to cool. When completely cool and firm, remove the sides of the pan and the paper strip (or strips) on the sides. Cover the cake with a rack and turn upside down. Remove the bottom of the pan and the paper lining on the bottom.

9. Place the cake upside down on a length of wax paper. Through a fine strainer, generously sprinkle on confectioners' sugar, forming a thick coating. Then carefully turn the cake right side up and sprinkle sugar on that side also. There should be a generous amount of sugar on both sides.

10. Wrap airtight in plastic wrap and let stand at room temperature for days, if you wish, or a week or two (or freeze).

11. To cut into portions, unwrap the room-temperature cake, re-sugar if necessary and using a long, sharp, heavy knife, cut straight down across the top. Then cut each half into eight wedges.

YIELD: 16 SERVINGS

Note:

You can use glazed fruit that you buy already diced, or you can buy the large pieces and dice them yourself. If you dice them yourself, cut the pieces about ¼-inch square.

You can also buy almonds that are already blanched and toasted.

BIBLIOGRAPHY

CO

Baker, Russell. *The New York Times,* "Fruitcake Is Forever," December 25, 1983.

Beard, James. *Delights and Prejudices: A Memoir with Recipes.* New York: Simon & Schuster, 1971.

Beranbaum, Rose Levy. *The Cake Bible.* New York: William Morrow, 1988.

Capon, Robert Farrar. *The New York Times,* "Fruitcakes: Solid Evidence of Christmas," December 14, 1983.

Capote, Truman. *A Christmas Memory.* New York: Random House, 1956. First published in *Mademoiselle,* 1956.

Child, Julia. From *Julia Child's Kitchen.* New York: Alfred A. Knopf, 1975.

Claiborne, Craig. *The New York Times,* "The Personal Touch on Holiday Fruitcakes," December 8, 1982.

Cunningham, Marion. *The Fanny Farmer Cookbook,* 13th edition. New York: Alfred A. Knopf, 1990.

Garmey, Jane. *Great British Cooking: A Well-Kept Secret.* New York: HarperPerennial, 1992.

Glen, Camille. *The Heritage of Southern Cooking.* New York: Workman Publishing Company, 1986.

Grigson, Jane. *English Food.* London: Macmillan, 1974; New York: Penguin, 1977.

Haedrich, Ken. *Ken Haedrich's Country Baking.* New York: Bantam Books, 1990.

Heatter, Maida. *Maida Heatter's Best Dessert Book Ever.* New York: Random House, 1990.

Idone, Christopher. *Glorious Food.* New York: Stewart, Tabori & Chang, 1982.

Lewis, Edna. "Fruitcakes for Christmas," *Gourmet,* October 1988, Condé Nast Publications, New York.

Loomis, Susan Hermann. *Farm House Cookbook.* New York: Workman Publishing Company, 1991.

Malgieri, Nick. *Great Italian Desserts.* Boston: Little, Brown & Company, 1990.

Neal, Bill. *Biscuits, Spoonbread and Sweet Potato Pie.* New York: Alfred A. Knopf, 1990.

Peck, Paula. *The Art of Fine Baking.* New York: Fireside Books, Simon & Schuster, 1961.

Pépin, Jacques. *The Art of Cooking, Volume II.* New York: Alfred A. Knopf, 1988, 1992.

Purdy, Susan. *A Piece of Cake.* New York: Macmillan/Atheneum, 1989.

Rosenberg, Judy. *Rosie's Bakery: All-Butter, Fresh Cream, Sugar-Packed, No-Holds Barred Baking Book.* New York: Workman Publishing Company, 1991.

Rosso, Julee, and Sheila Lukins. *The New Basics Cookbook.* New York: Workman Publishing Company, 1989.

Scharfenberg, Horst. *The Cuisines of Germany.* Bern: Hallwag AG, 1980; New York: Poseidon Press, 1989.

Smith, Jeff. *The Frugal Gourmet Celebrates Christmas.* New York: William Morrow, 1991.

Sorosky, Marlene. *Season's Greetings.* New York: HarperPerennial, 1986.

Steingarten, Jeffrey. "Jeffrey Steingarten cooks up the much-maligned fruitcake," *Vogue,* December 1991, Condé Nast Publications, New York.

Trillin, Calvin. *Enough's Enough.* New York: Ticknor & Fields, 1990.

Walter, Carole. *Great Cakes.* New York: Ballantine Books, 1991.

Welty, Eudora. "Holiday Greetings and Best Wishes for the Coming Year." Albondocani Press and Ampersand Books, 1980.

INDEX

e/o